H. W. JANSON AND THE LEGACY OF MODERN ART

AT WASHINGTON UNIVERSITY IN ST. LOUIS

This catalog was published in conjunction with
an exhibition at Salander-O'Reilly Galleries, New York
March 12–April 6, 2002
and at the Washington University Gallery of Art, St. Louis
August 30–December 6, 2002

Support for the exhibition was provided by
the Hortense Lewin Art Fund and Yeatman Art Fund
of Washington University

Editor: Jane E. Neidhardt, St. Louis
Designer: Martin Schott, New York
Printer: Dolan Wohlers, New Jersey

Co-published by Washington University Gallery of Art,
St. Louis, and Salander-O'Reilly Galleries, New York

Library of Congress catalog card number 2002141119
ISBN 1-58821106-1

Front and back covers:
Artworks in the Washington University Gallery of Art collection
(cat. nos. 1–20)

Spine:
Horst W. Janson, 1935
Reproduced from "Horst Woldemar Janson," by Lise Lotte
Müller, *Zeitschrift für Kunstgeschichte* 46, no. 4 (1983)

H. W. JANSON AND THE LEGACY OF MODERN ART

AT WASHINGTON UNIVERSITY IN ST. LOUIS

Sabine Eckmann

with contributions by
Bradley Fratello
George V. Speer

and

H. W. Janson

Washington University Gallery of Art, St. Louis
Salander-O'Reilly Galleries, New York

CONTENTS

FOREWORD

This exhibition of modern paintings and sculptures from the Washington University Gallery of Art in St. Louis was originally conceived as an opportunity to show a selection of the most important works of art in the Washington University collection in New York. Sabine Eckmann, curator of the Gallery of Art, took the opportunity provided by the exhibition to examine the formation of the University's collection of modern art in the 1940s, when H. W. Janson served as curator. In her essay Sabine Eckmann justifiably gives Janson a great deal of credit for building the University's modern collection. Janson was curator of the collection from 1944–1948 and as such was responsible for the selection of many of the objects owned by the University. Sabine Eckmann not only analyzes this central role Janson played in the arts at Washington University, but also uncovers some of the meaning these artworks held, for Janson and for the art world at large, in the politically turbulent times when they were acquired.

The story, of course, is more complex than Janson's contribution; the Washington University collection both predates and postdates his presence in St. Louis. Washington University is the home of the oldest art museum west of the Mississippi River, which began as part of the University's St. Louis School and Museum of Fine Arts, founded in 1881. From the beginning, the patrons of the University set out to provide the University and the St. Louis community with fine examples of new American and European painting and sculpture as well as examples of decorative and industrial art. As a result, the collection includes works by George Caleb Bingham, William Merrit Chase, Frederic Edwin Church, Thomas Eakins, Harriet Hosmer, George Inness, Jules Breton, Julien Dupré, Léon Lhermitte, Pierre Puvis de Chavannes, Joaquín Sorolla y Bastida, and many others.

Janson and his colleagues on Washington University's Art Collection Committee renewed the notion of collecting what is new. They collected from a specific point of view, which is the subject of Sabine Eckmann's essay. Such collecting inspired succeeding curators and directors, as well as a number of private collectors, to continue in the same vein. Hence, the current exhibition also includes a number of works purchased by or given to the University after Janson's departure. Succeeding directors and curators have continued to emphasize collecting contemporary art in addition to acquiring works that complement the already established collection. The Gallery of Art has strong holdings in the art of the post-World War II decades and is currently collecting work of the 1990s and beyond.

All the works displayed in the current exhibition and reproduced in this catalog stand on their own as masterpieces. We are proud to present them to you for your enjoyment.

As is always the case, the exhibition has been made possible through the hard work and contributions of a large number of people. In this case, the prime mover is and has been Larry Salander, who has given us the use of his gallery as a venue and has supported the project from the beginning. Andrew

Kelly and Andrew Butterfield have also been helpful in organizing the exhibition and assisting with the production of this book. In addition I thank the other members of the Salander-O'Reilly staff who helped make this project a reality.

At Washington University the entire Gallery of Art staff has worked hard on this project, as have many students at Washington University. M. Todd Hignite, graduate student in the Department of Art History and Archaeology, transcribed Janson's centennial address with the help of Ivana Salander, an undergraduate in the same department. Ivana also provided valuable assistance with research during the course of the project, as did undergraduate students Rachel Sloan and Caron Sain. Art History senior Andrew McDiarmid demonstrated commitment to the project beyond the call of duty in his finalization of provenance research and his work in obtaining photographs for the catalog. And graduate students Bradley Fratello and George V. Speer, who worked closely with Sabine Eckmann, contributed meaningfully to the scholarly value of this project with their research and writing of the catalog entries.

The staff of the Gallery of Art applied themselves as usual to the tasks at hand with a level of dedication and skill that made this endeavor, as with all of our projects and programs, possible. To them I extend my deepest thanks again, but I especially want to thank Jane Neidhardt, administrator of the Gallery of Art and editor of the catalog, whose professionalism, perceptive comments, and hard work advanced the quality of this book. In addition, assistant registrar Sara Rowe extended herself beyond the duties of her job to assist Jane Neidhardt with many aspects of the catalog.

It was my colleague, Sabine Eckmann, who took an idea and made it substantial. The success of both the exhibition and the catalog is largely the result of her efforts, and to her I extend my congratulations.

Mark S. Weil
Director, Washington University Gallery of Art

EXILIC VISION:

H. W. JANSON AND THE LEGACY OF MODERN ART

AT WASHINGTON UNIVERSITY

Sabine Eckmann

EXILIC VISION:
H. W. JANSON AND THE LEGACY OF MODERN ART
AT WASHINGTON UNIVERSITY

Sabine Eckmann

In June 1946 *Art News* critic Reed Hynds announced that Washington University in St. Louis had acquired "one of the finest collections of modern art to be found in the Midwest."[1] The heavily illustrated article assessed the University's new modern art acquisitions and discussed what are still considered some of the most important icons of modern art. These include Pablo Picasso's *Glass and Bottle of Suze* (1912; cat. no. 16), Juan Gris's *Still Life with Playing Cards* (*Draughts Board and Playing Cards*) (1916; cat. no. 9) and Max Beckmann's *Les Artistes mit Gemüse* (*Artists with Vegetable*) or *Four Men Around a Table* (1943; cat. no. 1). Within not much more than one academic year Washington University had purchased approximately forty twentieth-century artworks by European and American modernists. Little more than one-fifth consisted of American artworks. Hynds, although impressed by the fact that modern art was the main collecting emphasis at Washington University, criticized the selection for its dearth of American art. "Admirable as is the point of view that modern art is a world phenomenon, and the artist's point of origin has little relevance, the fact remains that there are some extremely significant American artists at work today who are not represented."[2] This evaluation positions Hynds, who was based as a cultural reporter at the St. Louis Post-Dispatch, in line with much of mainstream American art criticism of the time, which intended to strengthen the international reputation of the U.S. art world through stressing its indigenous aesthetic productions. In this way Hynds identified with many American modernists who attempted—in contrast to passionate and nationalistic anti-modernists—to inscribe modern American art into the European-dominated narrative of the modern movement. Yet the German dictatorship's public pillory of modern European art at the 1937 *Degenerate Art* exhibition played into the hands of influential American supporters of international modern art trends. Their alleged internationalism, however, revealed a pronounced predilection for modern European art. The most prominent of these American internationalists was Alfred H. Barr, Jr., then director of New York's Museum of Modern Art, whose response to the German dictatorship's pillory was to proclaim modern art the art of democracy, thereby attempting to establish ties between U.S. democracy and international modernism (figs. 2, 3).

1. Reed Hynds, "Yielding Place to New," *Art News* 45, no. 4 (June 1946): p. 32.
2. Ibid., p. 62.

Fig. 1
Horst W. Janson, 1935
Reproduced from "Horst Woldemar Janson,"
by Lise Lotte Müller, *Zeitschrift für Kunstge-*
schichte 46, no. 4 (1983)

3. See for example H. W. Janson, *Apes and Ape Lore in the Middle Ages and the Renaissance* (London: The University of London Warburg Institute, 1952).

4. See for example Janson, "Benton and Wood, Champions of Regionalism," *Magazine of Art* 39 (1946): pp. 184–86, 198–200.

H. W. Janson, who served as curator of the Washington University art collection from 1944 to 1948, was the instrumental force in selecting and acquiring modern art for the University. Having arrived in 1935 in the U.S. as an exile from Adolf Hitler's Germany, he rejected the National Socialists' nationalistic interpretation and propagation of German art and was committed to cosmopolitanism. Although he had become a naturalized American citizen in 1943 and enthusiastically participated in American academeme and the U.S. art world, his art historical methodology as well as his notions of modern art were shaped by German discourses. On the one hand, the so-called Hamburg School of art history—comprising primarily Jewish scholars like Janson's teacher Erwin Panofsky, who had developed iconography and iconology—had a lasting impact on Janson's own art historical scholarship.[3] On the other hand, Janson's perception of modern art was formed against the backdrop of the anti-modernist, racist and defamatory cultural policies of National Socialist Germany.[4]

By framing Janson as an exile from Nazi Germany within the U.S. art world of the 1940s, this essay will explore his concept of modern art as it is discernible in his acquisitions for Washington University and in his writings of the time. His particular exilic experience exposes various links between the German

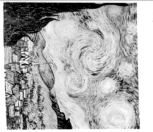

Fig. 2
Alfred H. Barr, Jr., c. 1929-30
Photograph courtesy the Museum of Modern Art, New York

Fig. 3
From *The Bulletin of the Museum of Modern Art: The Museum and the War*, vol. X (October–November, 1942): p. 19.
The Museum of Modern Art Library, New York
Photograph © 2001 The Museum of Modern Art, New York

culture from which he came and the new American culture. The essay will position Janson's agenda within the complex fabric of the 1940s U.S. art world and examine his concept of aesthetic modernism in relation to the broader reception of modern art at a time when debates over modernist versus anti-modernist and national versus international agendas governed the U.S. art world. The presence of many exiles from Europe–artists, art historians and art dealers–not only challenged the agendas of the U.S. modern art world but also heightened these debates. Responses to German racism, nationalism and anti-modernist aesthetics and the consequences for artistic production contributed to an anxious climate in which these issues gained momentous cultural and political significance.

About Exile

Today exile is seen as the quintessential experience of modernity and postmodernity. Throughout the past century totalitarian and authoritarian regimes forced into exile millions who are scattered around the world. Notions of exile range from an emphasis on exile as a fundamental loss, with the exilic life being one of marginalization and isolation (see the interpretations of Theodor W. Adorno and Bertolt Brecht, for example[5]), to perceptions of exile as a positive experience involving assimilation and productivity (as underscored by Edward Said and Vilém Flusser, among others[6]). Within the modernist discourse on exile the opposing poles–isolation on the one hand and assimilation on the other–play important roles. Exilic isolation is seen as furnishing an advantageous condition for an increase in creative productivity, while the experience of assimilation is viewed as leading to a reduction of artistic creativity.[7] This modernist dichotomy likens the exilic experience to the established notion of modernist artistic practice being positioned on the margins of society–a position that not only enables artistic creativity but also encourages criticality towards society. Apart from this correlation between modernism and exile, modernist productions that feature fragmentation and heterogeneity, such as Janson's acquisition of Picasso's *Glass and Bottle of Suze* (1912; cat. no. 16), can also be seen as reflective of the exilic experience because they lack a homogenous and unifying perspective.

Creativity and criticality connect these notions of exile and modernism to each other. The late philosopher Vilém Flusser, a Jewish exile to France from Nazi-occupied Prague, recently portrayed migration as both a creative endeavor and a suffering, but without embracing the trope of isolation. He characterized the exiled individual as having the potential to serve as an incubator for creativity produced in a climate of dialogue.[8] Although Flusser never immigrated to the U.S., his view was based on the European image of the U.S. that considers such metaphors of exile as homelessness, rootlessness, nomadism and unconnectedness to be essentially American qualities. "Indeed the new country is only for the expelled new land. Wherever he will be expelled to, there he will discover America. For the inhabitants who are supposed to receive him, it is the old country. Only the immigrant in America is factually an American,

5. Theodor W. Adorno, "Schutz, Hilfe und Rat," in his *Minima Moralia. Reflexionen aus dem beschädigten Leben*, 22nd ed. (Frankfurt am Main: Suhrkamp, 1994), pp. 32–34. Bertolt Brecht, "Sonett in der Emigration" in his *Die Gedichte von Bertolt Brecht in einem Band* (Frankfurt am Main: Suhrkamp, 1993), p. 831.

6. Edward Said, "Reflections on Exile," in *Out There: Marginalization and Contemporary Cultures*, ed. Russell Ferguson, Martha Gever, Trinh Minh-ha and Cornel West (New York, Cambridge, and London: Routledge, 1990), pp. 357–66. Vilém Flusser, *Von der Freiheit des Migranten. Einsprüche gegen den Nationalismus* (Bensheim: Bollmann, 1994).

7. See Karen Kaplan's analysis of this dominant modernist reading of exile in her *Questions of Travel: Postmodern Discourses of Displacement* (Durham and London: Duke University Press, 1996), esp. pp. 27–65.

8. Flusser, "Denn die Migration ist zwar eine schöpferische Tätigkeit, aber sie ist auch ein Leiden," in his *Von der Freiheit des Migranten*, pp. 17, 106.

and he is an American even if he should immigrate to ancient countries. Upon his arrival in exile he spreads out an American frame of mind. He becomes the epicenter of an earthquake, that the old inhabitants experience as upheaval of the usual. From the exile's point of view the opposite is at stake: he takes pains to make the unusual (namely, indeed, everything) habitable. This mutual misunderstanding might lead to a creative dialogue between the expelled and the old inhabitant."[9] Thus, according to Flusser, exilic production can be seen as a dialogical process that might lead to the creation of a new or different culture.

Translating these different notions of exile to Janson's situation–isolation, assimilation or dialogue–the parameters of his exile comprise various relations to old and new places of belonging. Both Weimar and Nazi German culture surfaced through different layers of memory in Janson's writings. In America he was exposed to a culture that was alien to him, but he had the potential to form a new culture in his new environment, rather than either acculturating himself to the existing one or remaining in isolation nostalgic of the world he left behind. Janson certainly attempted to embrace his new country from the beginning of his American life. The first letter he sent to his former colleague Lise Lotte Müller is signed "americanophilus."[10] How then would his concept of modern art reflect his new cultural position? Would he comprehensively promote all modern art in an oppositional response to the Nazis' pillory, including all modern American trends? Or would he exclusively embrace American art? Would Janson synthesize the American art world with the cultural baggage he brought with him from Europe, thus engaging in a dialogue as suggested by Flusser? And similarly, would his concept of modern art reflect a connection between exile and modernism, leading to a preference for aesthetic concepts that embrace fragmentation?

H. W. Janson

Horst Woldemar Janson (fig. 1) emigrated in 1935 from Hamburg, where he had studied art history. At the time of his arrival in the U.S., he was twenty-one years old. In Hamburg Janson had been a student of Erwin Panofsky, who, before being fired by the National Socialists from Hamburg University in 1933, had held guest professorships at Princeton University and New York University. Among Janson's fellow students in Hamburg were Lise Lotte Müller, William S. Heckscher and Lotte Brand Philip, the latter two of whom also immigrated to the U.S.[11] As gentiles, Janson and his fellow students left Germany voluntarily–to demonstrate loyalty to their Jewish teachers in defiance of the National Socialist racist policies.[12] Also indicative of Janson's aversion to Nazi Germany was his changing of his first name from Horst to Peter in response to the Nazi national anthem, called the Horst Wessel song. Wessel, who wrote the song, was a Nazi party member who was killed in 1930 by communist enemies of the Nazi movement and subsequently glorified as a Nazi martyr.[13]

9. Ibid., p. 106 (translation mine).

10. See Lise Lotte Müller, "Horst Woldemar Janson," Zeitschrift für Kunstgeschichte 46, no. 4 (1983): p. 466.

11. For more about the German art historical emigration during the Third Reich see Ulrike Wendland, Biographisches Handbuch deutschsprachiger Kunsthistoriker im Exil. Leben und Werk der unter dem Nationalsozialismus verfolgten und vertriebenen Wissenschaftler. 2 vols. (München: K.G. Saur, 1999) and Karen Michels, Transplantierte Kunstwissenschaft im amerikanischen Exil (Berlin: Akademie Verlag, 1999).

12. I thank Janson's son Anthony F. Janson for providing the information that Janson left Germany voluntarily after Panofsky was forced to flee.

13. Müller, "Janson," p. 466. Anthony Janson believes his father's changing of his name to have been simply an expression of his new American identity, and not a reaction to the Horst Wessel song.

14. There is contradictory evidence about whether Janson indeed received a grant through Erwin Panofsky, but Panofsky served–together with Wilhelm Köhler, a German art historian who held a professorship at Harvard University–on a committee to help young German scholars without national and international reputation to emigrate from Germany. See Michels, "Transfer and Transformation. The German Period of American Art History," in Exiles and Emigrés: The Flight of European Artists from Hitler, ed. Stephanie Barron and Sabine Eckmann (Los Angeles and New York: Los Angeles County Museum of Art and Harry N. Abrams, 1997), p. 307. According to Anthony Janson, Janson may have obtained a German government grant to study abroad via Harvard (letter to the author, April 4, 2001). Yet Wendland, author of Biographisches Handbuch, doubts that the German government granted study abroad fellowships at that time (letter to the author, March 3, 2001).

15. According to information provided by the Washington University News Bureau Biographical Report (October 10, 1944: Washington University archives), Janson obtained his degree in 1941. Other sources specify that he obtained his Ph.D. in 1942. See Wendland, Biographisches Handbuch, vol. 1, p. 332, and Müller, "Janson," p. 466.

16. Janson left Washington University in 1948 to accept a Guggenheim fellowship. One year later he was appointed Professor of Art History at New York University, a position he held until his retirement.

17. News Bureau, n.p.

18. Müller, "Janson," p. 468. Janson died in 1982 on a train ride between Zurich and Milan. Müller's obituary is one of the best sources for information about Janson's personality and career. For extensive bibliographic information see also Wendland, *Biographisches Handbuch*, vol. 1, pp. 332–38, and *Art, the Ape of Nature: Studies in Honor of H. W. Janson*, ed. Moshe Barasch and Lucy Freeman Sandler (New York and Englewood Cliffs, NJ: Harry N. Abrams and Prentice Hall, 1981), pp. 805–12.

19. See for example Janson's reviews on *The Sculptures of Michelangelo* by Ludwig Goldscheider, *Parnassus* 12 (1940): p. 31; *Academies of Art, Past and Present* by Antoine Pevsner, *Parnassus* 12 (1940): p. 25; *Studies in Iconology: Humanistic Themes in the Art of the Renaissance* by Erwin Panofsky, *Art Bulletin* 22 (1940): pp. 174–75.

20. Janson's articles include: "Karl Zerbe," *Parnassus* 13 (1941): pp. 65–69; "'Martial Memory' by Philip Guston and American Painting Today," *Bulletin of the City Art Museum of St. Louis* 27 (1942): pp. 34–41; "The International Aspects of Regionalism," *College Art Journal* 2 (1943): pp. 110–15; "Benton and Wood, Champions of Regionalism," *Magazine of Art* 39 (1946): pp. 184–86, 198–200; "The New Collection at Washington University," *College Art Journal* 6 (1947): pp. 199–206; "Philip Guston," *Magazine of Art* 40 (1947): pp. 54–58; "Karl Zerbe's Clowns," *The Magazine of the Year* 2, no. 6 (1948): pp. 80–81; "Max Beckmann in America," *Magazine of Art* 44 (1951): pp. 89–92. Janson's reviews include: *Alexander Calder* by James Johnson Sweeney, *College Art Journal* 4 (1945): pp. 64–66; *Pedagogical Sketch Book* by Paul Klee and *The Drawings of Paul Klee* by Will Grohmann, *College Art Journal* 4 (1945): pp. 232–35; *Artist in Iowa–A Life of Grant Wood* by Darrell Garwood, *Magazine of Art* 38 (1945): pp. 280–82; "Satirist's Dilemma," a review of *A Little Yes and a Big No* by George Grosz, *Saturday Review* 30 (1947): pp. 20–21; *Picasso–Fifty Years of his Art* by Alfred H. Barr, Jr., *College Art Journal* 6 (1947): pp. 315–17; *What Is Modern Painting?* by Alfred H. Barr, Jr., *Painting in Flanders* by Roberta M. Fansler and Margaret Scherer, and *Seven Painters–An Introduction to Pictures* by A. C. Ward, *College Art Journal* 5 (1946): pp. 256–59.

When Janson arrived on North American shores in 1935 to continue his art historical education at Harvard University as the Charles W. Holtzer Fellow, a position he possibly obtained through Panofsky,[14] he had already experienced significant physical displacement. Born in 1913 in St. Petersburg, Russia, his family had relocated to Hamburg, Germany after the 1916 upheavals of the October revolution in Russia. In 1932 Janson began his university education in Munich; one year later he transferred to Hamburg University. In 1938 he received his master's degree from Harvard University and in 1941 or 1942 completed his Ph.D. with a dissertation on "The Sculptured Works of Michelozzo di Bartolommeo."[15] Before accepting an assistant professorship at Washington University in St. Louis in 1941, Janson held an assistantship at the Fine Arts Department at Harvard University (1936–37), was instructor and lecturer at the Worcester Art Museum in Worcester, Massachusetts (1936–38) and lecturer at Iowa State University (1938–41).[16] In a 1944 Washington University News Bureau Biographical Report, Janson named as his fields of specialization Renaissance sculpture, medieval and Renaissance iconography and modern art.[17] Today Janson's international reputation still rests on his popular *History of Art* (1962), which by the time of his death in 1982 had been translated into fourteen languages and had sold more than 2.5 million copies.[18]

This essay, however, is primarily concerned with his writings of the 1940s. In addition to book reviews and essays on Renaissance art and art historical methodology,[19] Janson began publishing on modern art in 1941 with an essay on the Jewish-German modern artist Karl Zerbe, who immigrated to the U.S. in 1934. In the following decade, the period of his most prolific publication on modern art, Janson published articles on Beckmann, Picasso, George Grosz, Philip Guston and Paul Klee, as well as Thomas Hart Benton, Grant Wood and American regionalism.[20]

Implementing the Modern

In May 1945, the Art Collection Committee of Washington University, guided by Janson as both a member of the Committee and curator of the University Art Collection, embarked on the largest deaccessioning endeavor in the history of the University museum and sold more than one hundred and twenty paintings and five hundred pieces of "applied arts." The Art Collection Committee was chaired by Lawrence Hill, head of the School of Architecture. In addition to Janson, George Mylonas, chairman of the Department of Art History and Archaeology, and Kenneth Hudson, dean of the School of Art, were members of the Committee. The Committee submitted their acquisition and deaccession recommendations to the chancellor of the University. The University joined the City Art Museum (today The Saint Louis Art Museum), which had also decided to deaccession some of their artworks, auctioning off most at a public sale at Kende Galleries, New York. Roughly one-sixth of the entire collection of Washington University was dispersed through this auction. The most valuable artwork sold was Frederic S.

Remington's *A Dash for the Timber* (1889; fig. 33), which brought $23,000, more than half of the total proceeds from the sales ($40,000). In addition, the University sold paintings by nineteenth-century artists Rosa Bonheur, Dwight Tryon, Horatio Walker and others. Following Janson's advice, the Art Collection Committee acted swiftly and bought some forty paintings, sculptures and prints from European and American modernists. Most were purchased during the 1945–46 academic year, thereby establishing the first modern art collection at Washington University in a matter of months.[21] Although the collection was modest in size, the purchases amounted to the largest and most focused acquisition project the University had ever undertaken. Artworks such as Georges Braque's *Nature Morte et Verre (Still Life with Glass)* (1930; cat. no. 2), Theo van Doesburg's *Composition VII: The Three Graces* (1917; cat. no. 20), Max Ernst's *The Eye of Silence* (1943–44; cat. no. 7), Paul Klee's *Überbrückung (Transition)* (1935; cat. no. 11) and Joan Miró's *Peinture (Painting)* (1933; cat. no. 15) still form the core of the modern art collection. Moreover, this initial acquisition campaign stimulated subsequent acquisitions as well as important donations of modern art. In the 1950s and '60s, Janson's successors—among them Frederick Hartt and William N. Eisendrath, Jr.–and St. Louis art collectors Joseph Pulitzer, Jr., Morton D. May, Etta Steinberg, Sidney M. Shoenberg and Florence and Richard K. Weil, among others, added to the collection significant artworks of the time by such artists as Karel Appel, Jean Dubuffet (cat. nos. 5, 6), Eduardo Chillida, Sam Francis, Arshile Gorky (cat. no. 8), Willem de Kooning (cat. no. 4), Picasso (cat. no. 17), Jackson Pollock (cat. no. 18) and Antoni Tàpies. But they also rounded out Janson's project, adding, for example, cubist works by Jacques Lipchitz (cat. no. 12) and Braque, surrealist art by, among others, Miró (cat. no. 14), and expressionist paintings by Lyonel Feininger, Henri Matisse (cat. no. 13), and Chaim Soutine, and early American modernist canvases by Marsden Hartley (cat. no. 10) and Stuart Davis.[22]

The scope of the initial undertaking was unusual considering that modern art had become a major collecting emphasis of American museums only as recently as the late 1920s and 1930s. One could even call the project bold in light of the strong anti-modernist trends that then dominated the American art world, including university museums. For example, only two years earlier, Chancellor Chase of New York University, motivated by anti-modernist trends, had terminated the University's relationship with the prominent modern art collector, A. E. Gallatin, who had established the Museum of Living Art at that university. The collection included one hundred and seventy modern artworks by Picasso, Braque, Gris, Klee, Miró, Lipchitz, Fernand Léger, Jean Arp, Robert Delaunay, Marcel Duchamp, Piet Mondrian, Kurt Schwitters and Alexander Calder, among others. In turn, Gallatin gave the works to the Philadelphia Museum of Art.[23]

In a 1947 *College Art Journal* essay, Janson discussed the aims of the University museum.[24] He stressed the importance of reestablishing the Washington University Art Collection as a public institu-

21. One year earlier, in 1944, the University had purchased its first modernist prints, acquiring works by such artists as Pablo Picasso, André Derain, George Bellows, Camille Pissarro and Marie Laurençin.

22. See Joseph D. Ketner, "A Gallery of Modern Art at Washington University in St. Louis," in Ketner et al., *A Gallery of Modern Art at Washington University in St. Louis* (St. Louis: Washington University Gallery of Art, 1994), pp. 14–15.

23. M. R., "Living Art to Live in Philadelphia," *Art Digest* (February 15, 1943): p. 11.

24. Janson, "The New Art Collection at Washington University," *College Art Journal* 6 (1947): pp. 199–206.

Fig. 4
Givens Hall at Washington University in St. Louis

University Archives, Washington University in St. Louis

tion. The University museum was founded in 1881 as the St. Louis School and Museum of Fine Arts and a department of Washington University. Since 1905, however, the museum had not only, as Janson put it, "disappeared from public consciousness altogether," but was de facto defunct due to the lack of a building and public display space.[25] This first art museum west of the Mississippi, however, actively collected in the years surrounding the turn of the century, acquiring primarily applied arts and nineteenth-century American sculptures and paintings by such artists as Harriet Hosmer, George Caleb Bingham, Carl Wimar, Frederic Edwin Church and George Inness. In addition, nineteenth-century European paintings by moderate modernists, such as Gustave Brion, Jean-Baptiste-Camille Corot, Charles Daubigny and Léon Lhermitte, were added to the collection. The first four twentieth-century prints—by George Bellows, André Derain, Marie Laurençin and Picasso—entered the collection in 1944. That same year the Committee created a new exhibition space on campus in Givens Hall, which houses the School of Architecture (fig. 4). Hence the acquisition project deliberately coincided with the return of the University museum into the public sphere.

During the 1940s and early 1950s, Janson also repeatedly stressed the importance of making modern art accessible. While he clearly condemned the commodification of art and, like Clement Greenberg, defended modern art's elevated status, he nonetheless took a populist stance when it came to educating the general public about modern art.[26] For example, in a 1952 essay on documentary art films, he lauded the educational value of films about art, arguing for a close collaboration between filmmakers and art historians.[27] But Janson also expanded his educational agenda to encompass the popular arts. Already in 1944 he had initiated and organized a feature film series in collaboration with the City

25. The 1904 Palace of Fine Arts, erected for the World's Fair, was originally designated to house the University collection because the first museum building (the St. Louis School and Museum of Fine Arts, which had opened in 1881 in downtown St. Louis) had become too small. In 1906 Halsey C. Ives, the first museum director, indeed moved the collection into the Pavilion, which had been designed by renowned New York architect Cass Gilbert. In 1907 the citizens of St. Louis decided to tax themselves to support the new museum. This fund, however, was never released to the St. Louis Museum of Fine Arts, as it was a department of Washington University, a private corporation. As a result, the original University museum was dissolved in 1909, and the City Art Museum (today The Saint Louis Art Museum) was founded. For the next several decades the University collection remained on indefinite loan at the City Art Museum and was administered by its staff.

26. See Janson, review of *Artist in Iowa*, by Garwood, p. 282, and Clement Greenberg, "Avant-Garde and Kitsch" (first published in *Partisan Review* [Fall 1939]), in *Perceptions and Judgments, 1939–1944*, vol. 1 of *Clement Greenberg: The Collected Essays and Criticism*, ed. John O'Brian (Chicago and London: University of Chicago Press, 1986), pp. 5–22.

27. Janson, "College Use of Films on Art," in *Films on Art*, ed. William M. Chapman (Kingsport, Tenn.: 1952), pp. 38–52.

Fig. 5
Crowds queuing outside the exhibition,
Entartete Kunst (Degenerate Art), at the
Schulausstellungsgebäude Hamburg, 1938

28. Letters between Charles Nagel (then acting director of the City Art Museum while Perry Rathbone was on military duty) and Janson, July 3, July 18, and November 7, 1944 (The Saint Louis Art Museum archives). In a letter dated October 30, 1944, Janson suggested bringing Erwin Panofsky to St. Louis to lecture on film aesthetics (The Saint Louis Art Museum archives). On Panofsky and the founding of the Museum of Modern Art's film department see Thomas Y. Levin, "Iconology at the Movies: Panofsky's Film Theory," *The Yale Journal of Criticism* 9, no.1 (1996): pp. 27–55.

29. Janson, review of *What Is Modern Painting?* by Barr, pp. 256–68. See also Janson, "Letters on the Education of Artists in Colleges," *College Art Journal* 4 (1945): p. 213.

Art Museum. The prints of the films were borrowed from the Museum of Modern Art's recently founded film department. In a similar vein, in 1946 he had reviewed Alfred H. Barr, Jr.'s booklet *What Is Modern Painting?*, which was intended to expand the general public's knowledge of modern art. In his review Janson even went so far as to discuss the appropriate sale price of the publication to ensure its broadest dissemination.[29] This concern with the accessibility of modern art in both its high and low manifestations must also be read against the background of the Nazis' success in pilloring modern art. Largely, their victory was contingent upon the German general public's very limited understanding of modern art. Indeed, the Nazis grounded their nationalistic and racist propaganda against modern art in the popular concept of art as craftsmanship that accomplishes its goal through an accurately rendered and skilled imitation of visible reality. This concept, together with the denouncement of modern art as elitist, was cleverly utilized in the 1937 touring exhibition *Degenerate Art* to convince the German public of the inferiority of modern art. The exhibition was attended by more than three million visitors, making it one of the best-visited of all modern art exhibitions (fig. 5).

According to Janson, the objectives of Washington University's acquisition project were threefold: to prioritize the educational mission of the institution by targeting the student body of the University; to avoid duplications with the City Art Museum's collection; and to assemble a body of artworks representative of the modern movement, with each work valuable as an individual creation as well. In line with these goals, Reed Hynds confirmed in his *Art News* article that "the general intention was simply to present as complete a view of the developments of modern art as was possible."[30] Yet Janson's limited funds of $40,000 certainly made a complete representation of the modern movement an unrealistic aspiration. By comparison, in 1942 New York's Museum of Modern Art had an annual acquisition fund of approximately $80,000.[31] Moreover, the market for contemporary art peaked in 1945. Sales had steadily increased since 1940 and during the 1945–46 season, when Washington University entered the market, there was a 37% increase in prices over 1944.[32] Thus Janson's acquisitions must be considered in light of these economic limitations.

The majority of artworks acquired in 1945 and 1946 date from the 1930s and 1940s, a period of twentieth-century art that is still marginalized within the established narrative of modernism. Nevertheless, the new collection comprised artworks by many leading European modernists such as Beckmann, Braque, van Doesburg, Ernst, Gris, Léger, Klee, Miró, Picasso and Antoine Pevsner. To represent American modernists the selection fell to Calder, Davis, Guston, William A. Baziotes and Joseph Stella, among others. Cubism was illustrated through works by Picasso, Braque, Gris and Stella, and constructivist tendencies by van Doesburg, Pevsner, Léger and Jean Hélion. Surrealism was exemplified with works by Baziotes, Calder, Ernst, Klee, Miró, Roberto Sebastián Antonio Matta Echaurren, Henry Moore and Yves Tanguy, and figurative positions that vacillate between expressionist, neo-romantic and realist traditions were advanced by Beckmann, Guston, Zerbe and Eugene Berman. Yet many of these works would fit multiple categories. Overall, Janson's selection of modern art demonstrates a strong emphasis on cubism, constructivism and surrealism in exile and is complemented by an array of contemporary European modernists with their American counterparts, thereby mixing the old world with the new. Yet surprising in Janson's selection is the relative lack of modern German art. German expressionism is only represented by one print each by Grosz (fig. 28), Ernst Barlach and the Austrian Oskar Kokoschka, none of whom had been core members of either the Bridge group in Dresden or the Blue Rider group in Munich.[33] The only major work by an artist who held strong affiliations to the German Bauhaus is Klee's geometric and abstract painting *Überbrückung* (1935; cat. no. 11). Yet, due to the Nazis' much publicized pillory, modern German aesthetic practices were in the limelight in the U.S. and many German artworks were available on the American art market.

Promoting the Modern

The artworks that Janson acquired were almost exclusively purchased in New York, the newly proclaimed center of the modern art world.[34] Most of the dealers from whom he purchased modern art not only had well-established reputations, but were exiles from Europe, and it was due to their efforts that

30. Hynds, "Yielding Place," p. 62.

31. A. Deirdre Robson, *Prestige, Profit, and Pleasure: The Market for Modern Art in New York in the 1940s and 1950s* (New York and London: Garland Publishing, Inc., 1995), p. 30.

32. Aline B. Louchheim, "Second Season of the Picture Boom: Private Buying of Contemporaries Continues to Climb," *Art News* 44, no. 10 (August 1945): pp. 9–12.

33. The three lithographs are *The Execution (Kein Hahn Nach Ihnen)*, 1927, by George Grosz; *Portrait of the Artist's Mother*, 1917, by Oskar Kokoschka; and *Der tote Tag (The Dead Day)*, 1912, by Ernst Barlach.

34. Harold Rosenberg, "Fall of Paris," *Partisan Review* (December 1940): pp. 440–48.

20

important European artworks were available. Most exile dealers maintained strong connections to Nazi Europe, and despite complications were able to receive shipments from Europe during and immediately after the war. Important purchases Janson made from exile dealers and professionals closely connected to their circle include Calder's *Bayonets Menacing a Flower* (1945; cat. no. 3), Beckmann's *Les Artistes mit Gemüse* (1943; cat. no. 1) and Henry Moore's *Reclining Figure* (1933; fig. 39) from Curt Valentin's Buchholz Gallery, and Braque's *Nature Morte et Verre* (1930; cat. no. 2) and Hélion's *Rouge Brilliant* (1938; fig. 6) from Paul Rosenberg. The French expatriate Pierre Matisse (the son of Henri), who had settled in New York in the early 1920s, sold Miró's *Peinture* (1933; cat. no. 15), Tanguy's *La Tour Marine (Tower of the Sea)* (1944; cat. no. 19) and the early twentieth-century New Guinea sculpture *Homme Oiseau* (c. 1900; fig. 38) to Washington University, while van Doesburg's *Composition VII: The Three Graces* (1917; cat. no. 20) and Pevsner's *Bas Relief en Creux (Sunken Bas Relief)* (1926–27; fig. 40) were acquired from the American expatriate and avant-garde collector Peggy Guggenheim, then back in New York. The American Julien Levy, who had in the early 1930s introduced Americans to surrealism, remained exclusively committed to promoting surrealist work and emphasized exile artists in particular. From him Janson purchased Ernst's *The Eye of Silence* (1943–44; cat. no. 7) as well as Matta's *Lambeaux Iron-Oniriques (Iron-Oneiric Scraps)* (1942; fig. 7). Léger's *Les Grands Plongeurs (The Divers)* (1941; fig. 8) came from Valentine Dudensing, who, since the mid-1920s, had established a reputation for dealing in modern European art. In the 1940s he supported exile artists Léger and Mondrian.

21

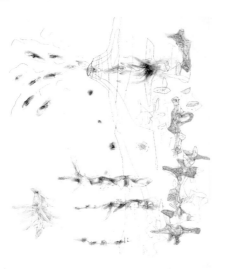

Although these dealers all gave priority to modern European art, their agendas differed. Some were committed to modern German art banned in its homeland, others focused on French art and the surrealists in exile, and some–to a limited degree at least–integrated contemporary American art into their program. Differentiating their agendas will not only demonstrate how they penetrated the contemporary American art world and which sets of aesthetic, cultural and political interests they pursued, but will also place Janson's purchases within this web, thereby illuminating his own interests.

The majority of modern artworks in the Washington University art collection were purchased from Curt Valentin. He was trained by Daniel-Henry Kahnweiler in Paris and Alfred Flechtheim in Berlin and immigrated to the U.S. in 1937 because of his Jewish ethnicity. There he established the Buchholz Gallery, first on 46th Street and then in 1939 on 57th Street (fig. 9). This neighborhood soon became a "tight bot-

35. "57" Street: A Tight Bottleneck for Art in the United States," *Fortune* 34 (September 1946): pp. 145–49.

36. Valentin opened the Buchholz Gallery in 1937 with the exhibition *Sculpture and Drawing*, from March 18 to April 17, which included works by Barlach, Kolbe, Lehmbruck, Marcks, Scheibe and Sintenis. This was followed by the *Exhibition of Beckmann, Hofer, Kirchner, Klee, Macke, Nay, Nolde, Scholz, Barlach, Kolbe, Marcks, Sintenis*, from May 10 to June 4, 1937 (Curt Valentin Archives, Museum of Modern Art, New York).

tleneck" of the leading galleries for modern art.[35] Valentin actively promoted modern German art, in particular expressionism, and was the foremost dealer to sell German art to museums and private collectors throughout the country. At first in New York he continued to feature what had been his main focus in Germany—namely, sculptures and works on paper.[36] But over the next four years his emphasis shifted toward one-man shows of persecuted German artists, such as Ernst Ludwig Kirchner, Klee and Beckmann, in an attempt to establish a new market for their work. His altered agenda coincided with an increase in the knowledge of, and interest in, modern German art that resulted from the infamous 1937 *Degenerate Art* exhibition (fig. 10). Earlier, Alfred H. Barr, Jr.'s 1931 exhibition *German Painting and Sculpture*, along with the efforts of German expatriate dealers such as I. B. Neumann, who had founded his New York gallery New Art Circle in the mid-1920s, had slowly prepared the ground for the reception of modern German art in America at a time when strong anti-German sentiments dominated U.S. perceptions after World War I. Valentin's professional relationship with the owner of his New York gallery, the German art dealer Karl Buchholz, enabled Valentin to offer important German artworks, many formerly in German museums, as Buchholz was a member of the Nazi party and confiscated modern art for the German government. Such artworks by Beckmann, Kirchner, Kokoschka, Franz Marc and Emil Nolde were included in the 1940 exhibition *Landmarks in Modern German Art*, which comprised nineteen paintings and seven sculptures. The text for the exhibition brochure was prepared by Perry T. Rathbone, who later that year became director of the City Art Museum and who as curator at the Detroit Institute of Arts had been exposed to modern German art by its director, the German art historian

Fig. 9
Curt Valentin in his Buchholz Gallery, New York City, c. 1940s
Jane Wade Papers, 1903–1971, Archives of American Art, Smithsonian Institution

Fig. 10
Review of the exhibition *Degenerate Art*, from "Pogrom of Art," by Morrill Cody, *The Digest* 1, no. 6 (August 21, 1937): p. 9.

Figs. 11, 12
Pages from *Artists in Exile*, exhibition brochure (New York: Pierre Matisse Gallery, 1942)

The Pierre Matisse Gallery Archives, Gift of the Pierre Matisse Foundation, 1997. The Pierpont Morgan Library, New York, MA 5020
Artists in Exile photograph by George Platt Lynes, 1942

Left to right, first row: Roberto Sebastián Antonio Matta Eschaurren, Ossip Zadkine, Yves Tanguy, Max Ernst, Marc Chagall, Fernand Léger. *Second row:* André Breton, Piet Mondrian, André Masson, Amédée Ozenfant, Jacques Lipchitz, Eugene Berman. *Third row:* Pavel Tchelitchev, Kurt Seligmann.

William Valentiner. In this text, Rathbone emphasized the importance of German art by foregrounding its aesthetic value. "But in consequence of the undreamt fate that has overtaken modern German art in the land of its origin, this exhibition has a unique distinction: all of the paintings and most of the sculptures have been the property of eleven German museums. Thus the exhibition represents the collective critical judgement of a museum personnel which was remarkable for its foresight and independence in the prompt recognition of the importance of contemporary German art, and was in a position to secure the best and most significant works–the landmarks of the movement."[37] In line with Rathbone's arguments that validated the quality of the artworks by pointing to the authority of German curators, Valentin kept his interpretation of modern German art apolitical, and even went so far as to decline an exhibition on German exile art because of its political implications.[38] Valentin's reliance on autonomous aesthetic value contributed to his success in the U.S. art world and was a strategy that served him especially well during the years leading up to America's entry into World War II, when public statements against the German regime were discouraged.[39] And although Valentin remained committed to modern German art throughout the 1940s, he began adding French modernists–such as the newly arrived exiles André Masson, Lipchitz and Léger–to his program, paying tribute to the American preference for the work of the ethnically diverse Parisian artists.[40] It was from this later addition to Valentin's program that Janson made most of his selections. Given the fact that Valentin was, and remained, the country's foremost dealer in German expressionism, the absence of such works in Janson's "representative" selection of modern art is all the more surprising.

37. Perry T. Rathbone, *Landmarks in Modern German Art*, Buchholz Gallery exhibition brochure, 1940 (Curt Valentin Archives, Museum of Modern Art, New York), n.p.
38. Valentin to Ernst Ludwig Kirchner, January 13, 1938 (Curt Valentin Archives, Museum of Modern Art, New York).
39. Ibid. Valentin's correspondence with Kirchner also demonstrates his neglect of politics: Kirchner accused Valentin of showing the work of Emil Nolde, a member of the Nazi party. Another example of downplaying politics in the U.S. is the exclusion from a George Grosz exhibition in 1935, by Harvard University's Germanic Museum (today the Busch-Reisinger Museum), of artworks by Grosz that criticize the Nazis (curator Charles L. Kuhn to collector Erich Cohn, October 1935 [Busch-Reisinger Museum archives]).
40. During this time Valentin held contacts with the German-Jewish art dealer Daniel-Henry Kahnweiler, who had fled persecution in Paris and moved to the unoccupied French countryside. Kahnweiler had urged Valentin to represent André Masson in the United States (Valentin to Lily Klee, September 10, 1941 [Curt Valentin Archives, Museum of Modern Art, New York]).

41. The exhibition included works by surrealists André Breton, Max Ernst, André Masson, Matta, Kurt Seligmann and Yves Tanguy, as well as works by Marc Chagall, Fernand Léger, Piet Mondrian and Jacques Lipchitz, all of whom had emigrated from France to America.

In contrast to Valentin, Pierre Matisse featured exile artists as a group, publicizing their presence in New York and raising awareness of the changed conditions of production for artists in France and the state of modern French art. In 1942 he organized the widely reviewed exhibition *Artists in Exile* (1942; figs. 11, 12).[41] In the accompanying exhibition brochure, American James Thrall Soby, curator at the Museum of Modern Art, published an essay entitled "Europe," while Nicolas Calas, the Greek surrealist exile writer who came to the U.S. from France, wrote on "America." Both articles stressed the tension between the newly arrived European exile artists and American artists. Soby and Calas took stances against nationally oriented discourses on art and instead advocated international artistic exchanges. Yet Matisse's own gallery program remained exclusively devoted to modern French art. Thus his investment in cross-cultural collaboration appears as a pretense to championing the exile artists that had formed Paris as the capital of the art world. His program included Marc Chagall, Tanguy, Matta and Léger, as well as some who had chosen to remain in Europe: Picasso, Miró and Georges Rouault, for example. In several major exhibitions Matisse traced the interface between politics and art and actively promoted the art of Paris. *War and the Artist* (1943) explored the impact of World War II on modernist artistic production in France, and *Salon d'Automne* (1944) celebrated the first Salon de la Liberation in Paris after the war and acknowledged the limitations placed on artistic production in Vichy, France during the occupation. No other French dealer in New York was so dedicated to modern French art. Paul Rosenberg, for example, who had fled France in 1940 and opened his New York gallery in 1942, never politicized his program. He downplayed the division between American and European artists and the Nazis' cultural pillory of modern art, although much of his own collection had been looted by the Nazis. While in France his main focus had been impressionist and post-impressionist art, as well as the work of Picasso. In the U.S. he added cubists such as Braque, who had formerly been represented by Rosenberg's brother Leonce. Briefly during the 1940s Rosenberg also exhibited some American artists whose work demonstrated formal ties to French art, such as Max Weber, Abraham Rattner and Hartley.

Janson's most important link to a dealer whose program combined both exile and American artists was Peggy Guggenheim, an American Jew who had been living in Europe for two decades until she was forced to leave in 1941. Upon her return to New York she continued her plans to build an unconventional museum, for which she hired the innovative Austrian exile architect Frederick Kiesler (fig.13). Her permanent collection featured a surrealist gallery and one devoted to non-objective and constructivist aesthetic modes. Yet Guggenheim's focus did not remain limited to modern European art. She actively embraced new American art, initiating a dialogue between both cultures. From 1943 to 1947, she held an annual spring salon of young American artists that was juried by major European exiles, including Mondrian and Duchamp.[42] She was also the first dealer to feature Pollock, Baziotes and Robert Motherwell in one-man exhibitions.

The presence of these exile and expatriate dealers strengthened the market for modern European art in New York, a development that was often perceived as a threat to American art and its market. Dealers such as Valentin, Rosenberg and Matisse were much attached to the art they had brought from the old world; they fought hard to win the American market and succeeded. Established prejudices that valued America as the country of modernity but without modernist culture played to their advantage. Guggenheim's reputation among professionals in the New York art world was contested. She was regarded more as an eccentric celebrity than a serious art professional, but in fact was the only one to engage both national groups with one another at a time when both perceived themselves as marginalized, Europeans because of their displacement and Americans because of the lack of support for their art.

These tendencies formed the basis for Janson's agenda of modern art. He rejected the latest American expressionistic abstractions—as conveyed in works by Pollock and Gorky and promoted by Guggenheim—even though he purchased Baziotes' abstract but more constructive composition *Still Life* (1945; fig. 35) from Samuel Kootz, who would emerge as one of the most important early promoters of the future abstract expressionists.[43] In 1947, Janson made clear his rejection of pure American abstract art—and implicitly criticized its main promoter, Clement Greenberg—in a characterization of Guston's work: "[Guston] instinctively distrusted advocates of pure form, who rejected any hint of representation as 'commercial art.'"[44] Janson's ventures into the American art world led to purchases of primarily figurative works—such as Guston's *If This Be Not I* (1945; fig. 37) and Yasuo Kuniyoshi's

42. Peggy Guggenheim was also the first one to address contemporary women artists in an exhibition in 1943.

43. In addition to Guggenheim, Howard Putzel (who had worked for Guggenheim and then established his own Gallery 67) and Samuel Kootz were engaged supporters of the new American abstract art.

44. Janson, "Philip Guston," p. 55. See also Greenberg, "Avant-Garde and Kitsch," pp. 5–22, and Janson, "'Martial Memory' by Philip Guston," pp. 34–41.

45. See Robson, "Dealers," in her *Prestige, Profit, and Pleasure*, pp. 77–128.

46. Gustav Hartlaub, director of the Mannheim Kunsthalle in the 1920s, coined the term Neue Sachlichkeit in 1923. In 1925 he organized at the Mannheim Kunsthalle the pivotal exhibition *Neue Sachlichkeit–Deutsche Malerei seit dem Expressionismus* (*New Objectivity–German Painting since Expressionism*). In 1933 he was dismissed by the National Socialists.

47. Janson, "International Aspects of Regionalism," p. 113.

Tomorrow Will Come (1945; fig. 14)–and ones that reveal ties to modern French art, such as Calder's organic and surrealist *Bayonets Menacing A Flower* (1945; cat. no. 3) and Stella's cubist *Man in the Elevated (Train)* (1918; fig. 34). Most of these purchases were made from such galleries as Midtown, Downtown and Charles Egan, all of which were entirely devoted to American art and had been active centers for modern American art since the 1920s. Midtown Gallery had organized Guston's New York debut in 1945.[45]

In contrast to Valentin, as well as to German exile art historians–including Alfred Neumeyer at Mills College and Alexander Dorner at the Rhode Island School of Design–Janson did not stress modern German art as a primary collecting goal, a fact that bespeaks Janson's deliberate distance from his previous German culture. Despite his impassioned defense of modern art in general, his acquisition program did not involve a rehabilitation of the pilloried German expressionists, dadaists or Bauhaus artists. On the contrary, he even harshly denounced Weimar Germany's most advanced contemporary realistic art, termed Neue Sachlichkeit, or New Objectivity, for nationalistic traits.[46] "Since it represented a departure from artistic ideas that had originated in France, the Neue Sachlichkeit inevitably acquired a strong nationalistic tinge. Many of its converts, after dabbling in Cubism or Expressionism in earlier years, justified their change of heart by denouncing these styles as foreign 'isms' and by professing to have rediscovered the 'heritage of German painting.'"[47] In this rejection of Neue Sachlichkeit, Janson alluded to the more conservative paintings of such artists as Georg Schrimpf (fig. 15), who, in contrast to socially and politically engaged artists Grosz, Otto Dix and Christian Schad, for example, took a seemingly affirmative stance towards society, often featuring simple everyday objects and harmonic German landscapes or cityscapes untouched by modernity. Instead, Janson voiced his interest in the allegedly more cosmopolitan trends advanced by the Paris art world and executed not only by such French artists as Braque, Léger and Tanguy, but by many foreign artists who had chosen Paris as their home, including

Fig. 14
Yasuo Kuniyoshi (American, b. Japan, 1889–1953)
Tomorrow Will Come, 1945
Brush and ink, 28⁹/₁₆ x 22¹/₂"
Washington University Gallery of Art,
St. Louis, University purchase, Kende Sale
Fund, 1946
© Estate of Yasuo Kuniyoshi/Licensed by VAGA,
New York, NY

Ernst, Matta, Picasso and Miró. Even though Janson preferred modern French art over modern German art, his acquisitions of works by Moore, Pevsner, van Doesburg and American modernists detached him from Matisse's national agenda.

Rational Modernism

Janson's endeavor to represent the early twentieth-century modern art movement was focused on cubist and constructivist approaches. Among the works he collected that demonstrate such rationally oriented aesthetic agendas are two early cubist works—the 1912 collage *Glass and Bottle of Suze* (cat. no. 16) by Picasso and the 1916 Gris painting *Still Life with Playing Cards* (cat. no. 9)–and a later cubist painting by Braque, *Nature Morte et Verre* (1930; cat. no. 2). The latter work complements the City Art Museum's work by Braque, *The Blue Mandolin* (1930; fig. 16), which was acquired by the Museum in January of 1945 from the Paul Rosenberg Gallery.[48] Although the Washington University painting is of considerably smaller dimensions, it could be argued that in this particular case Janson, in contrast to the goals of the acquisition program, duplicated the City Art Museum's holdings.[49] In this sense the purchase of *Nature Morte et Verre* particularly speaks to Janson's strong commitment to cubism. In line with the analytical and constructive tendencies that characterize cubism's semi-abstractions–especially the tendency to break homogenous depictions of the visible world into heterogenous fragments–are Janson's purchases of the constructivist works *Composition VII: The Three Graces* (1917; cat. no. 20) by van Doesburg and Pevsner's *Bas Relief en Creux* (1926–27; fig. 40). Artworks of the 1930s and 1940s, such as Hélion's *Rouge Brilliant* (1938; fig. 6), Léger's *Les Grands Plongeurs* (1941; fig. 8), Baziotes' *Still Life* (1945; fig. 35) and, to a certain extent, Klee's *Überbrückung* (1935; cat. no. 11), all subscribe to modernist agendas that value rational approaches distinct from the highly subjective and emotional works of German expressionism.

48. *St. Louis Star-Times,* January 6, 1945 (The Saint Louis Art Museum archives). Washington University's Braque painting was also purchased from Rosenberg.

49. Paul Klee's *Überbrückung* in the Washington University collection is arguably also closely related to The Saint Louis Art Museum's painting by Klee, *Polyphonic Architecture* (1930), acquired in 1942 by its director Perry Rathbone from Karl Nierendorf in New York City.

50. Alfred M. Frankfurter, "The Model of a Major Modern Collection," *Art News* 44, no. 9 (July 1945): pp. 28, 34, 35.

51. Alfred H. Barr, Jr., *Cubism and Abstract Art*, exh. cat. (New York: Museum of Modern Art, 1936). The dust jacket of the catalog shows Barr's famous chart, "The Development of Abstract Art."

52. Barr, reprinted in *Defining Modern Art: Selected Writings of Alfred H. Barr, Jr.*, edited with an introduction by Irving Sandler (New York: Harry N. Abrams, 1986), p. 90.

53. The Museum of Modern Art held a widely reviewed retrospective of Miró's work in 1942. He was featured together with his Spanish colleague Salvador Dali.

54. Barr, *Defining Modern Art*, p. 16.

In July of 1945, when Janson started his acquisition program, Alfred M. Frankfurter, the editor of *Art News*, reviewed Alfred H. Barr, Jr.'s new installation of the Museum of Modern Art's permanent collection, entitling his article "The Model of a Major Modern Collection."[50] In the new installation Barr singled out cubism as the most important early twentieth-century movement by placing cubist works at the center of the installation and flanking them with constructivist artworks with their origins in cubism. The connection between cubism and constructivism was a concept Barr had already foregrounded in 1936 in *Cubism and Abstract Art*, an exhibition in which he explored the development of abstract art in the twentieth century along formalist lines (fig. 17).[51] In the accompanying catalog he stated that "the first and more important current [of modern art] finds its sources in the art and theories of Cézanne and Seurat, passes through the widening stream of Cubism and finds its delta in the various geometrical and Constructivist movements. . . . This current may be described as intellectual, structural, architectonic, geometrical, rectilinear and classical in its austerity and dependence upon logic and calculation."[52]

Eight years later the historical importance of cubism and abstract art of the 1910s and 1920s to the development of the modern art movement was reinforced by Sidney Janis in his 1944 book *Abstract and Surrealist Art in America*. These critical evaluations of early twentieth-century modernism had significant impact on the internationalists in the 1940s American art world, who were already predisposed toward modern French art and artists who formed the international art world in Paris.[53] In 1940 the authority of modern French art was again emphasized by Barr, who noted in an assessment of contemporary American art that "painting and sculpture [are] two fields in which America is not yet, I am afraid, quite the equal of France. . . ."[54] Similarly, in 1946, when the Whitney Museum of American Art mounted the exhibition *Pioneers of Modern Art in America*, its curators, Lloyd Goodrich and Hermon

Fig. 16
Georges Braque (French, 1882–1963)
The Blue Mandolin, 1930
Oil on canvas, 45 5/8 x 34 7/8"
The Saint Louis Art Museum, Purchase
© 2001 Artists Rights Society (ARS), New York/ADAGP, Paris

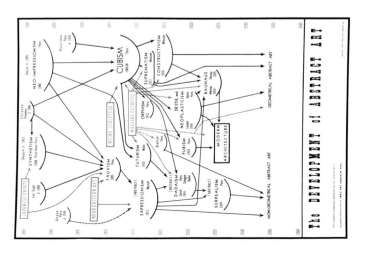

Fig. 17
Revised version of chart prepared by Alfred H. Barr, Jr. for the jacket of the catalog of the exhibition *Cubism and Abstract Art*, The Museum of Modern Art, New York, 1936

Photograph © 2000 The Museum of Modern Art, New York

More, only displayed French precursors of American modernism, emphasizing in particular cubism.[55] Thus Janson's focus on cubism, the art of Paris and constructivist aesthetic tendencies drew upon the concepts of enormously influential American art historians and institutions.

Yet Janson's writings suggest that he did not follow Barr without cause. Telling in this regard is Janson's 1945 review of the English translations of Klee's *Pedagogical Sketch Book*, published by Karl Nierendorf, and Will Grohmann's *The Drawings of Paul Klee*, published by Curt Valentin. Janson discussed Klee's work–often seen solely as playful and poetic creations indebted to the unconscious–as rationally oriented yet pseudo-scientific conceptions, in accordance with Klee's exploration of artistic principles drawn from mathematics, physics and biology. He underscored that Klee "believed his art to be communicable and subject to rational analysis to a greater extent than many of his admirers have been willing to admit."[56] This statement alludes to Grohmann's book, which Janson generally assessed in positive terms but criticized for its characterization of Klee's work according to stereotypical notions of the artistic genius–notions that Janson saw as referring less to the nineteenth-century concept of the artist's extraordinary individuality than to the organic, mythic and de-individualized portrayal of artistic creation as propagated by Nazi ideology. In his review of this work, Janson particularly repudiated Grohmann's interpretation that Klee's genius "recall[s] primitive darkness of which fragments still live in the artist" and Grohmann's assessment that "there are no visible turning points in [Klee's] career, for he lives and works out of a fixed center," instead arguing for an objective art historical analysis.[57] Janson's

55. Frankfurter, "O Pioneers! The Whitney Examines the Pathfinders of Modern Art in America." *Art News* 45, no. 2 (April 1946): pp. 34–36, 65.

56. Janson, review of *Pedagogical Sketch Book by Klee* and *Drawings of Klee* by Grohmann, p. 233.

57. Ibid., p. 234.

58. For an illuminating article on Grohmann's involvement with the Nazi regime see Monika Wucher, "Dr. Grohmanns Empfehlungen. Leitmotive moderner Kunstpublizisik im Nationalsozialismus," in *Überbrückt. Ästhetische Moderne und Nationalsozialismus. Kunsthistoriker und Künstler 1925–1937*, ed. Eugen Blume and Dieter Scholz (Köln: Verlag der Buchhandlung Walther König, 1999), pp. 109–23.

59. See Stefan Germer, "Kunst der Nation. Zu einem Versuch die Avantgarde zu nationalisieren," in *Kunst auf Befehl? Dreiunddreissig bis Fünfundvierzig*, ed. Bazon Brock and Achim Preiß (München: Klinkhardt & Biermann, 1990), p. 27.

criticism illuminates his deep scepticism towards an irrationalism that centers imagination and artistic creation in elemental forces, the necessity of natural laws and the nature of the "volk" as alluded to by Grohmann. Grohmann, an early supporter of Wassily Kandinsky, Ernst Ludwig Kirchner and Klee in the 1920s and one of the most influential promoters of abstract and progressive art during the early decades of the Federal Republic of Germany, continued his career without a break throughout the Third Reich. After his admission into the Nazi-controlled Reich Literary Chamber (Reichsschrifttumskammer) in 1936, he published frequently in such Nazi publications as the *Neue Linie* (New Line), *Das Reich* (The Reich) and *Die Pause* (The Break). In all of these writings he subscribed to National Socialist ideology, stressing irrational concepts and describing artistic works as products of instinct, intuition and emotion, blending blood and soil with racist and nationalistic ideologies.[58] However, Grohmann's book about Klee (written in 1934) was confiscated by the Nazis, who persecuted Klee as a modernist. In the early 1930s Grohmann, like other German art historians (such as Werner Haftmann[59]), attempted to join modern German art to Nazi ideology by underscoring its nationalistic Germanness and blood and soil elements–elements emphasized by Grohmann in his analysis of Klee's art. Alois Schardt, director of Berlin's Kronprinzenpalais from 1933 to 1934, installed the museum's permanent collection in 1934 to prove to the Nazis that German expressionism embodies "Germanic art's will," stressing its irrational qualities that he contrasted to the supposed rationality of French art. In this way Schardt highlighted a semblance between German expressionism and National Socialism. For Janson, who surely remembered the 1933–34 attempts to link modern German art with Nazi ideology, irrationalism connoted not only the blood and soil ideology already popular with the youth movement at the turn of the century, but

Crowds at the Picasso Art Show

The Pablo Picasso art exhibit at the City Art Museum attracted a large number of visitors yesterday. This group is viewing the "Guernica" mural, which is twenty-five feet, eight inches long and eleven feet, six inches high and was painted as a protest against the bombing of the town of Guernica, Spain, during the Spanish Civil War.

Fig. 18
From a review of the exhibition *Picasso: Forty Years of his Art* (*St. Louis Star-Times*, March 18, 1940)

also Germanness. His criticism of Grohmann's interpretation of Klee appears partly born of his resistance to Nazi ideology. Hence Janson's affinity for aesthetic rationality is grounded in two discourses. First, it is a response to Nazi aesthetics (that repudiated intellectualism in favor of propagating a collective, elementary creativity lying outside the individual's control) and their nationalistic and racist concepts of Germanness. Second, it corresponds to the American art world's belief that cubism and constructivist, non-objective tendencies were historically the most important currents of the modern art movement.

While the art world in Nazi Germany subscribed to radicalized nationalism and racism, the American art world witnessed vehement debates over international modernism versus national regionalism. For example, in 1939 the Museum of Modern Art organized an exhibition, *Picasso: Forty Years of his Art*, that traveled to the City Art Museum (among many other venues), where it was the most publicized exhibition of the decade (fig. 18). There it received mixed reviews that reflected the larger debate over international and modern art.[60] Much of this debate concerned the issue of an indigenous modern American art detached and independent from modern European trends, which were becoming increasingly available to the public as more and more renowned European artists, such as Ernst, Tanguy, Léger and Duchamp, were arriving on American shores as exiles. On the one hand, internationalist Samuel Kootz, an early supporter of such abstract expressionists as Mark Rothko and Baziotes, argued in his 1943 book *New Frontiers in American Painting* that American culture should follow Franklin Delano Roosevelt's anti-isolationist politics to inspire a cosmopolitan art. On the other hand, critics such as Peyton Boswell, who regularly wrote the editorials for *Art Digest*, took an isolationist and nationalistic stance when it came to guiding American art into a successful future.[61] The common concern of both was the conquest of American art over European culture. Harold Rosenberg, who, together with Clement Greenberg, emerged as one of the main supporters of abstract expressionism, already in his 1940 article "The Fall of Paris" had suggested that the U.S. could now take over leadership of the art world so long dominated by Paris. While Rosenberg, Greenberg and Kootz mark the most advanced positions to support a radical modern American art of international ambition, at the other end of the spectrum were conservative forces, such as the Sanity in Art movement that promoted well-crafted naturalistic artworks celebrating America, its soil and its people. While the nationalistic positions generally favored anti-modernist and American trends, the internationalists also embraced modern European art.

Janson emerged in this discourse with his essays "The International Aspects of Regionalism" (1943) and "Benton and Wood, Champions of Regionalism" (1946), and a review of Darrell Garwood's *Artist in Iowa – A Life of Grant Wood* (1945). In the latter Janson compared the art of American regionalists Wood and Benton to Germany's Neue Sachlichkeit and Nazi art, claiming that collectively, German paintings such as Georg Scholz's 1925 *Ansicht von Grötzingen bei Durlach* (fig. 19) resemble official

60. Among other reviews see: "Largest Exhibit by a Single Artist Examined for Flaws by Art Museum Registrar," *St. Louis Post-Dispatch*, March 7, 1940; "Women as a Spanish Artist Sees Them," *St. Louis Globe-Democrat*, March 10, 1940; "Crowds at the Picasso Art Show," *St. Louis Star-Times*, March 18, 1940; "Picasso Nerts, or Is He the Nerts," *St. Louis Globe-Democrat*, March 17, 1940; "It's a Blitzkrieg in Painting' Says Artist of Picasso Exhibition," *St. Louis Star-Times*, March 16, 1940; "Arresting and Imposing Exhibit of Picasso's Art at City Museum," *St. Louis Globe-Democrat*, March 17, 1940; "Picasso Art Show Is Enormous–Be it Good or Bad," *St. Louis Star-Times*, March 16, 1940. (All available in The Saint Louis Art Museum archives.)

61. See Peyton Boswell, *Modern American Painting* (New York: Dodd, Mead & Company, 1939).

32

62. Janson, "International Aspects of Regionalism," pp. 110–15; review of *Artist in Iowa* by Garwood, pp. 280–82; "Benton and Wood," pp. 184–86, 198–200.

Fig. 19
Georg Scholz (German, 1890–1945)
Ansicht von Grötzingen bei Durlach (*View of Grötzingen near Durlach*), 1925
Oil on canvas, 27³/₄ x 39⁷/₅"
Städtische Kunsthalle Mannheim

Permission to reproduce granted by Friedel Scholz

Fig. 20
Werner Peiner (German, 1897–1984)
Die deutsche Erde (*The German Soil*),
c. 1933–45
Location unknown

Reproduced from *Die Malerei im Deutschen Faschismus: Kunst und Konterrevolution*, by Berthold Hinz (München: Wilhelm Heyne Verlag, 1974)
© 2001 Artists Rights Society (ARS), New York/VG Bild-Kunst, Bonn

Fig. 21
Grant Wood (American, 1891–1942)
Fall Plowing, 1931
Oil on canvas, 30 x 40"
Courtesy of the John Deere Art Collection

Nazi art, such as Werner Peiner's *Die deutsche Erde* (*The German Soil*) (c. 1933–45; fig. 20), as much as they do American regionalist paintings such as Wood's *Fall Plowing* (1931; fig. 21).[62] By foregrounding this visual likeness, Janson asserted that Nazi art, German realism of the 1920s and American regionalism are all inherently nationalistic. He characterized these paintings as naturalistic renderings using calculated compositions that lack imagination and stress craftsmanship. But Janson's comparison did not rely solely on formal features; he also compared these works in terms of their underlying ideological agendas. National Socialism propagated its ideology by relying on such dichotomies as nationalism versus internationalism, anti-intellectualism versus intellectualism, rural anti-modernity versus urban modernity. By exploring Wood's and Benton's writings of the mid-1930s—in particular Wood's *Revolt Against the City* (1935) and Benton's *An Artist in America* (1937), in which both argue

that American art should be detached from French artistic domination in favor of national and regional particularities–Janson singled out their preferences for the "rural," "unsophisticated," "normal" life that they contrasted to the unhealthy and intellectual life of the city. By underscoring in their writings the same anti-modernist and nationalistic arguments the Nazis disseminated, Janson established a connection between Nazi art and ideology and American regionalism.[63] Of course there are limits to this comparison, as racism, extreme irrationalism and radicalized nationalism (as communicated through Nazi art and instrumentalized by the Nazis for political purposes) were not part of the American regionalists' agenda. However, the common threads of anti-modernism and nationalistic traits were reason enough for Janson to aggressively and repeatedly take a public stance against the regionalists. And even though Wanda Corn has convincingly demonstrated that Wood never intended to depict contemporary America as a rural society in an anti-modernist idiom, but instead used midwestern nineteenth-century scenes to celebrate rural America in a timeless approach, one can still see Wood as embracing America in a nationalistic manner.[64]

Participating in a symposium on "The State of American Art" published in the *Magazine of Art* in 1949–four years after the military defeat of Nazi Germany–Janson pointed out that "the whole question of 'American style' smacks strongly of cultural nationalism and is in danger of involving extra-artistic criteria."[65] Janson illustrated his contribution to the symposium–which was introduced by Robert Goldwater and included such authorities as Alfred H. Barr, Jr., Jacques Barzun, Holger Cahill, Clement Greenberg and James Thrall Soby–with Wood's *Dinner for Threshers* (1934; fig. 22) as an example of the American art he despised. Also illustrated was Guston's *The Tormentors* (1948), a semi-abstract composition that strongly alludes to the horrors of World War II. Guston was among those American contemporary artists that Janson valued highly. His painting *If This Be Not I* (1945; fig. 37), which Janson acquired for Washington University, is a more precisely rendered composition than *The Tormentors.* It uses allegorical devices to address the inhumanity of the time. In 1942 Janson had published on Guston's *Martial Memory* (1941), a painting acquired by the City Art Museum that same year.[66] In this essay and in an essay on Guston that Janson published in 1947 in the *Magazine of Art,* he spelled out the reasons for his positive assessment. In 1947, a year after Guston had received the

63. Janson, "International Aspects of Regionalism," pp. 112–13; and Janson, "Benton and Wood," pp. 185–86.

64. Wanda Corn, "The Birth of a National Icon: Grant Wood's American Gothic," in *Art, the Ape of Nature,* pp. 749–69.

65. Janson, "A Symposium: The State of American Art," *Magazine of Art* (March 1949): p. 96.

66. Janson, "'Martial Memory' by Philip Guston and American Painting Today," *Bulletin of the City Art Museum of St. Louis* 27 (1942): pp. 34–41.

67. Janson, "Philip Guston," p. 55.
68. In addition to Guston, Janson saw Alexander Calder, whose *Bayonets Menacing a Flower* he acquired in 1945, as the best example of an American contemporary artist of international importance. According to Janson, Calder merged American characteristics such as "humor, irreverence, and mechanical ingenuity" with the art of Mondrian and Miró "into an integrated and highly original style" (Janson, review of *Alexander Calder*, p. 65).

Carnegie Prize and shortly before he began to create abstract compositions, Janson read him as an ally in his disapproval of American scene painting, social realism and pure abstract paintings, the last strongly advocated by Greenberg.[67] But, in contrast to Greenberg, Janson saw in Guston's later paintings (which combined constructive formal elements with allegorical and realistic aspects) signs of an artist who could solve the dilemma of American art and create works that would stand in their own right independent of modern European art. According to Janson, Guston found inspiration in the works of Picasso, Miró and archaic and "primitivist" art as well as in American modernity, the last, in Janson's eyes, embodying technical progress. He categorized Guston as an intellectual modernist who emphasized the German art historical notion of "Materialgerechtigkeit"–the use of the canvas as a carrier of a picture that respects its own qualities as a two-dimensional device and that may denote reality on a more symbolic or universal level. At the same time, Janson stressed that the surfaces of Guston's paintings recall modernist collages and thus negotiate the "conflict of modern man." For Janson, modernity's fragmented and disrupted perception of life as made transparent in collages certainly echoed his own experience as an exile. Janson's evaluation of Guston is based on the one hand on European culture, the exile experience and ties between Guston's work and artworks of the European avant-garde of the 1910s. On the other hand it is grounded in his view of American modernity. Both European and American influences, according to Janson, are synthesized in Guston's work into a new visual image that is rendered distinct from so many other contemporary practices through the unique imagination of its creator.[68]

Clearly Janson sought in Guston his own concept of modern art: he saw Guston's art as international, negotiating European and American sources, and as avoiding outright political content, instead transposing important contemporary issues onto a higher plane. Lastly, Janson highlighted Guston's art as modernist in its treatment of the dissociated experience of modernity and constructivist in its formal appearance. Overall, Janson's concept of modern art demonstrated a strong rejection of nationalism, irrationalism and anti-modernism that is based on his condemnation of Nazi ideology. This condemnation led Janson to a predilection for French art and rational aesthetics, which were seen by influential American art historians as instrumental to the development of modern art.

Exile Art

In addition to Janson's interpretation of artworks in terms of their rational aesthetics, he also collected exile art. Sometimes these two projects overlapped. For example, *Les Grands Plongeurs* (1941; fig. 8) by French exile Léger demonstrates a clear tectonic design that structures the interpenetration of the divers' bodies, a theme Léger embraced while in Marseille waiting for passage to America. Yet many of Janson's other acquisitions, in particular works by the exiled surrealists Ernst, Tanguy, Matta and Stanley

Fig. 23
Reuben Kadish (American, b. 1913)
Job, 1945
Engraving with aquatint, trial proof,
12 ³/₁₆ x 17 ³/₄"
Washington University Gallery of Art,
St. Louis, University purchase, Kende Sale
Fund, 1946

Fig. 24
Andre Racz (American, b. Romania, 1916)
Perseus Beheading Medusa, VIII, 1945
Engraving with aquatint, 7/25,
26 ¹/₁₆ x 18 ¹/₄"
Washington University Gallery of Art,
St. Louis, University purchase, Kende Sale
Fund, 1946

69. See Romy Golan, "On the Passage of a Few Persons through a Rather Brief Period of Time," in *Exiles and Émigrés*, pp. 134–42.

70. Eleanor Jewett, "Art Institute's Surrealism Show Opens June 29," *Chicago Sunday Tribune*, May 31, 1942, p. 4.

71. Greenberg, "Surrealist Painting" (first published in *The Nation* 159, nos. 7, 8 [August 12 and 19, 1944]), reprinted in *Perceptions and Judgments*, pp. 225–31. In reference to figurative elements, Greenberg observed, for example, that "Ernst's volcanic landscapes look like exceptionally well-manufactured scenic postcards" (ibid., p. 229). In reference to abstract forms and colors, Greenberg noted, for example, Matta's "iridescent burlesque-house decorations . . . which are little more, really, than the comic strips of abstract art" (Greenberg, "Review of Mondrian's *New York Boogie Woogie* and Other *New York Boogie Woogie* and Other New Acquisitions at the Museum of Modern Art" [first published in *The Nation*, October 9, 1943], reprinted in *Perceptions and Judgments*, p. 154).

72. *Art Digest*, Nov 1, 1942.

William Hayter, exemplify the engagement of modern art with processes of creation that involve the unconscious and the irrational. In 1940 Hayter had relocated his print studio, Atelier 17, from Paris to New York's New School for Social Research. There it developed into a center of inventive printmaking based on surrealist principles of automatism involving both European exiles and American artists. The success of this endeavor led in 1944 to *Hayter and Studio 17: New Directions in Gravure*, an exhibition organized by the Museum of Modern Art that consisted of more than sixty prints by thirty-one artists, including Masson, Calder, Lipchitz and Chagall. Janson purchased examples of this cross-cultural collaboration, including such prints as Reuben Kadish's *Job* (1945; fig. 23) and Andre Racz's *Perseus Beheading Medusa, VIII* (1945; fig. 24). And with the acquisition of Ernst's *The Eye of Silence* (1943–44; cat. no. 7), Tanguy's *La Tour Marine* (1944; cat. no. 19) and Matta's *Lambeaux Iron-Oniriques* (1942; fig. 7), examples of exile art representing the most advanced contemporary voices were added to the Washington University collection.

During the 1940s, Ernst, Matta and, to a lesser degree, Tanguy were encountering contradictory responses in the national art press. On the one hand, they were lauded as illustrious celebrities and major European surrealists.[69] On the other hand, they were harshly criticized by anti-modernists. For example, Ernst's work was characterized as "perverse, unhealthy, abnormal," conjuring Nazi attacks on modern art.[70] In addition, Clement Greenberg commonly assessed their works negatively as "commercial art" due to their figurative elements and considered them kitsch, seeing in them colors and forms reminiscent of American popular culture (e.g., comic strips).[71] Nevertheless, these exiles established their reputations in the New York art world. In 1942 *Art Digest* reported on New York shows being dominated by works of surrealists.[72] That same year, several exhibitions—such as *First Papers of Surrealism* at the Whitelaw Reid Mansion in Manhattan (fig. 25) and *Artists in Exile* at the Pierre Matisse Gallery—

73. Parker Tyler, "The Amorphous and the Fragmentary in Modern Art," Art News 44, no. 10 (August 1945): p. 18.

74. See André Breton, "Matta" (1944), reprinted in his Surrealism and Painting (New York: Harper and Row, 1972), p. 187.

75. Greenberg, "Surrealist Painting," The Nation, pp. 192-93, 219-20.

Fig. 25
Marcel Duchamp (American, b. France, 1887–1969)
Installation for the exhibition First Papers of Surrealism, October 14–November 7, 1942, Whitelaw Reid Mansion, New York
Philadelphia Museum of Art: Marcel Duchamp Archives, Gift of Jacqueline, Peter and Paul Matisse in memory of their mother, Alexina Duchamp
Photograph by John D. Schiff
© 2002 Artists Rights Society (ARS), New York/ADAGP, Paris/Estate of Marcel Duchamp

as well as the opening of Peggy Guggenheim's gallery-museum Art of This Century highlighted the exiles' contributions to the modernist movement. By 1946, exiled artists had become an integral part of the New York art world just as many of them returned to Europe. Janson's interest in surrealism may have been stimulated by these works' fragmented portrayals of the visible world that in the 1940s were traced back to cubism, particularly centering on Picasso's accomplishments, by critics such as Parker Tyler.[73] Yet Janson must have also harbored scepticism toward the surrealist protest against the rationalism of civilization and the movement's consistent investment in irrationalism and the unconscious. For that matter it is important to take into account that André Breton, surrealism's main theorist, demonstrated interest, during his exile in New York, in artistic concepts related to science, indicating at least to a certain degree a departure from surrealism's exclusive involvement in the psychological and unconscious. For example, Breton supported the young Chilean artist Matta, whose artistic concept was focused on morphology and who wanted to create an art that depicted the constantly shifting forms of an object or a phenomenon.[74] This receptiveness to concepts that approximate rationalism must have attracted Janson to surrealism. Furthermore, even though by now we are used to the narrative that constructs surrealism in exile as a precursor of abstract expressionism, the discourse of art criticism during the 1940s entertains different readings. Perhaps most significantly, Greenberg rejected surrealism in 1944 as a progressive art movement on the grounds of its literary subject matter and its populism.[75] However, Janson, as discussed earlier, advocated the broadest dissemination of modern art and was interested in the translation of object-derived subject matter into the field of visual language. Surrealist images (such as Ernst's The Eye of Silence), while rooted in representation, offer multiple meanings to be encoded by a critical viewer. Lastly, and more generally, if we follow Janson's modernist thought process–rooted in such dichotomies as modernism versus anti-modernism and nationalism versus inter-

nationalism—surrealism endorsed in more than one way Janson's agenda: surrealism's incoherent renderings of fragments of reality, or elements that allude to objects, distinguish the movement clearly as modern, and the composition of the group and their 1920s and 1930s celebration of the condition of deterritorialization mark surrealism's international character.

However, Janson's writings on exile do focus on German art. He published essays on "Karl Zerbe" (1941), "Karl Zerbe's Clowns" (1948), and "Max Beckmann in America" (1950), as well as "Satirist's Dilemma" (1947), a review of George Grosz's autobiography *A Little Yes and a Big No*.[76] Janson also purchased two paintings by German exile artists: Beckmann's *Les Artistes mit Gemüse* (1943; cat. no. 1) and Zerbe's *The Armory* (1941; fig. 26). While the Beckmann canvas was executed during the artist's Amsterdam exile in 1943 and emphasizes the spiritual life among materially deprived modern artists in exile, Zerbe's *The Armory* alludes to the persecution of modern art in Nazi Germany and America's entry into World War II. In North American scholarship both artists are often linked to the German expressionist movement, although their paintings have more in common with Germany's New Objectivity movement. Relative to expressionist works, these paintings rely upon a more unsentimental

76. See n. 20.

77. Janson, "Beckmann in America," p. 89.
78. Janson, "Karl Zerbe," p. 66.
79. Ibid.

mode of depiction realized through a static pictorial structure that includes a reduction of gestural elements and a heightened naturalism.

Janson's definition and concept of exile and the exilic experience are developed in his essays on Beckmann and Zerbe. He differentiated forced exile from voluntarily exile, defining the first as encompassing racist and political persecution that renders emigration a matter of life or death, while the latter he saw as comprising the free decision to leave Nazi Germany on grounds that could range from political and ideological antipathy toward the regime to the simple motivation to pursue a career as a modern artist. Within this scheme, Janson identified Beckmann's Amsterdam refuge as "self-imposed exile" in contrast to the forced exile of Zerbe, who emigrated from Germany to the U.S. in 1934 due to his Jewish ethnicity.[77] Janson's engagement with exile also resulted in a social and cultural analysis of the relationship between the exile and the exile's new home. He pointed to the necessity of the exile artist to assimilate with her or his new environment while simultaneously acknowledging the difficulties of this endeavor. "[The exile artists'] plight often seemed to mock the truth of the generally accepted dictum that the language of art is the most international of tongues. All of them had to adjust themselves to the unaccustomed physical setting, the new cultural climate, the artistic tradition, and the conditions of patronage in this country, and at times the ensuing conflicts have produced a genuinely tragic situation."[78] In contrast to a concept that situates artistic production in isolation or in a transcendental realm, Janson described a web that entangles artistic production in the public sphere, seeing the specific cultural, political and social environment as much a part of the artwork as is the artist's individuality. Seemingly taking his own biography as a point of departure, Janson gave younger artists without international acclaim a better chance to succeed with their new bodies of work conversant with the new culture than he gave established artists. The situation of established artists would be particularly challenging, Janson believed, as the U.S. public would expect a continuation of their acclaimed European artworks, while the artists, contingent on the new environment for new production, would create work different than audience expectations. But if these artists produce work similar to what they had created in their former country, Janson predicted their "style would soon be debased to empty routine."[79] Janson's concept of the exilic condition and artistic production defines the new environment as a public sphere that is consequential for creativity, discarding the possibility of an artistic position completely isolated from a specific cultural and political context.

For Janson, exile art is thus never purely a transfer but will always embrace transformation. In contrast to both German and U.S. postwar interpretations of exile art that claim exile as national inheritance, Janson avoided national fixations and envisioned cross-cultural fertilization. He characterized both Zerbe and Beckmann as successful exiles, detecting in their works traces of their new environment that are blended with their earlier German artistic practices. Yet in reviewing Grosz's autobiography A Little Yes

Fig. 27
George Grosz painting *Cain* (1944),
New York
© Bildarchiv Preussischer Kulturbesitz, Berlin

Fig. 28
George Grosz (American, b. Germany,
1893–1959)
*The Execution (Kein Hahn Kräht Nach
Ihnen)*, 1927
Lithograph, 16 ⅛ x 12 ¼"
Washington University Gallery of Art,
St. Louis. University purchase, Kende Sale
Fund, 1946
© Estate of George Grosz/Licensed by VAGA,
New York, NY

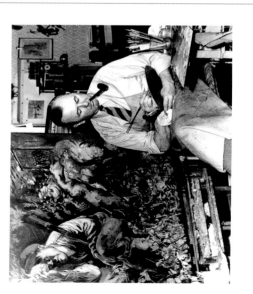

and a Big No, Janson portrayed Grosz's exile as the displacement of an involuntary exile in America who desired an American identity. Elaborating on Grosz's cynicism towards modernism, his idealizations of his American life, his resistance to the politics of the Third Reich, and the artist's nostalgia for the time before World War I, Janson accounted for Grosz's inability to create the new life he desired for himself (fig. 27). Reflecting on Grosz's political artwork, Janson, like many contemporary and later critics, observed that "as a newcomer to this country, Grosz simply was not sufficiently at home in the social and political scene of America" to create the kind of social-critical artworks that he had in Weimar Germany.[81] Janson added that Grosz could not criticize his new country in the way he had attacked his former harsh criticism of German society and politics "since that would have condemned him to the ... hopeless existence of a perpetual exile" on account of his lack of engagement with the U.S.[82] Instead of selecting an exile artwork by Grosz for the Washington University collection, Janson bought the lithograph entitled *The Execution (Kein Hahn Kräht Nach Ihnen)* (1927; fig. 28) from Grosz's Weimar years.[83]

Unlike with Grosz's work, Janson identified elements in both Zerbe's and Beckmann's American oeuvres that mirrored their new culture. Beckmann (fig. 29) had been unable to obtain a visa to move to the U.S. until 1947. While Janson believed that much of Beckmann's American work "perpetuates the

80. Janson, "Satirist's Dilemma," pp. 20–21. In this review of Grosz's *A Little Yes and a Big No*, Janson also states his disdain for Salvador Dali, who, at the time, was the most celebrated exile in the United States (see Eckmann, "Salvador Dali," in *Exiles and Emigrés*, pp. 148–55; and Golan, "On the Passage of a Few Persons through a Rather Brief Period of Time," ibid., pp. 138–40). For a discussion of Grosz's exile in America see Eckmann, "George Grosz," ibid., pp. 285–95, and Barbara McClosky, "George Grosz in den USA: Kunst und Anti-Stalinismus in den dreißiger Jahren" and Birgit Möckel, "*A Little Yes and a Big No: George Grosz in Amerika*," in *George Grosz: Berlin–New York*, exh. cat., ed. Peter-Klaus Schuster (Berlin: Staatliche Museen zu Berlin–Preussischer Kulturbesitz, Ars Nicolai, 1994), pp. 279–82, 283–98.

81. Janson, "Satirist's Dilemma," p. 20. For Grosz's contemporary reception, see Eckmann, "George Grosz," pp. 293–94.

82. Ibid.

83. Although this lithograph is dated 1927, in comparison with Grosz's oeuvre and considering the subject matter, it is more likely that the work dates from the time of the November Revolution or shortly thereafter, i.e., c. 1919–1921.

Fig. 29
Max Beckmann, 1949
University Archives, Washington University in St. Louis

Fig. 30
Max Beckmann (German, 1884–1950)
Fisherwomen, 1948
Oil on canvas, 75 1/4 x 55 1/4"
The Saint Louis Art Museum, Bequest of Morton D. May
© 2001 Artists Rights Society (ARS), New York/VG Bild-Kunst, Bonn

Fig. 31
Max Beckmann (German, 1884–1950)
Self-Portrait in Blue Jacket, 1950
Oil on canvas, 55 1/8 x 36"
The Saint Louis Art Museum, Bequest of Morton D. May
© 2001 Artists Rights Society (ARS), New York/VG Bild-Kunst, Bonn

tragic violence of the preceding years," he also wrote of the "self-contained architectural stability of design" in the Fisherwomen (1948; fig. 30), the "new American sense of scale" in his landscapes, and Beckmann's pragmatic view of himself in Self-Portrait in Blue Jacket (1950; fig. 31), seeing these as aspects of a dialogue Beckmann conducted with his new country.[84] Apart from the freedom-promising vast scale of the American landscape, Janson's categorization of American elements in the work of Beckmann are connected to notions that identify the U.S. with advanced modernity. In this way the American characteristics emphasize the rationalism of modernity. This argument resembled the assessment Janson had made eleven years earlier of Zerbe's work as an exilic dialogue. In light of Janson's generational theory, Zerbe, who arrived in the U.S. at age thirty-one, was an ideal subject for study. The

84. Janson, "Beckmann in America," pp. 90, 92.

German-American art historian acknowledged some links between Zerbe's work and cubism, but positioned Zerbe's work squarely between German expressionism and New Objectivity, seeing in the artworks a fusion of both.[85] Beginning in 1936, an additional element of "structural clarity"–as realized, for example, in Washington University's *The Armory* (1941; fig. 26)–entered his work and was synthesized with his earlier pictorial practice. This structural clarity, in Janson's eyes, was reflective of advanced modernity, a quality that had commonly shaped Weimar German intellectuals' perception of America as an embodiment of technological progress. In this sense, structural clarity marked the American element in Zerbe's work while still being anchored in earlier, European-derived approaches.

Janson also saw Zerbe's subject matter vacillating between the two cultures. In his 1948 essay "Karl Zerbe's Clowns," Janson read the artist's clown images (fig. 32) as metaphors of the crises of modern man. These outcasts of society that Janson saw embodied in the modern artist would typify the individual's loss of autonomy in both Germany and the U.S. The clown theme commonly appeared in many paintings since the 1920s, including in canvases by Beckmann, Picasso and Rouault.[86] Later observers have regarded this theme as a concession to the artist's political and societal powerlessness,[87] as if in response to Janson's 1948 question of how to retain one's identity as an individual against the crushing pressure of mass movements and mass psychology.[88] Mass culture was common to both Nazi Germany's dictatorial regime and the advanced capitalist structures of the U.S. The notion of liquidating the autonomous individual in the affirmative mass cultures of post-liberal America and totalitarian Germany had led philosophers Theodor W. Adorno and Max Horkheimer to write their *The Dialectic of Enlightenment* (1944). The Frankfurt School philosophers emphasized that rationality used in an instrumentalized form, as they detected it in Nazi and American industrialist mass culture, may lead to irrationalism, as mass culture's deceptiveness and conforming demands threaten individual autonomy. In contrast to Adorno and Horkheimer, Janson's criticism of mass culture was based less on Marxist critique than on liberal values that defended the subject's individuality and were grounded in the belief in an enlightened rationality. However, many resemblances are irrefutable. Like Adorno and Horkheimer, Janson was against the commodification of culture and in favor of highly individualized aesthetic creations. He also objected to a conservative, elitist criticism of mass culture. This was evident in his many attempts to make modern art as accessible as possible.[89]

Conclusion

When Janson's acquisitions of 1945 and 1946 for Washington University (some forty artworks) are seen together with his contemporary writings on modern art, it becomes apparent that his interpretations of modern art are grounded in both German and U.S. discourses. As an engaged defender of modern art and a harsh critic of German and American anti-modernist movements, Janson took a

85. Janson, "Karl Zerbe," p. 68.

86. See Cornelia Homburg, "Beckmann and Picasso," in *Max Beckmann and Paris: Matisse, Picasso, Braque, Léger, Rouault*, exh. cat. (St. Louis, Zurich, and Cologne: The Saint Louis Art Museum, Kunsthaus Zürich, and Taschen, 1999), pp. 52–59.

87. See Benjamin Buchloh, "Figures of Authority, Ciphers of Regression: Notes on the Return of Representation in European Painting," *October* 16 (Spring 1981): pp. 39–68, reprinted in *Art After Modernism: Rethinking Representation*, ed. Brian Wallis (New York and Boston: The New Museum of Contemporary Art and David R. Godine, Publisher, Inc., 1984), p. 118.

88. Janson, "Zerbe's Clowns," p. 77.

89. See for example Janson's comment, "As the skeptics have pointed out, the current marriage of art and industry is indeed an uneasy one" ("Benton and Wood," p. 200). He also declared that "modern art must not be made dependent on mass appeal. . . . In our age of standardized mass responses, his [the artist's] existence as the champion of individual experience and self-realization is becoming increasingly precarious. This problem of survival is as acute in Europe today as it is in America: whether it can be solved depends on the future course of Western civilization as a whole" ("State of American Art," p. 96).

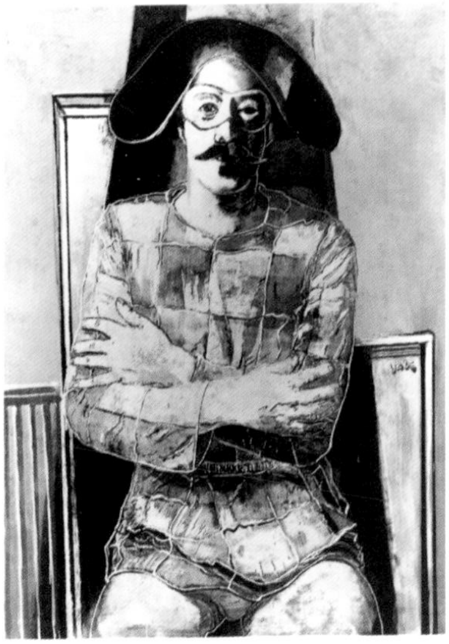

strong stance against national fixities. While Nazi Germany practiced radicalized nationalism, the U.S. art world also engaged in competing notions of national investments. On the one hand exile dealers such as Curt Valentin and Pierre Matisse demonstrated a significant degree of identification with the art and culture of their country of origin, and their marketing of modern German and modern French art were read in national terms. On the other hand, national discourses also dominated modern American art as modernists and anti-modernists alike attempted to establish the importance of an endemic American art that ran counter to the interest of such defenders of internationalism as Alfred H. Barr, Jr. Yet, in contrast to Barr, Janson stressed the role of cultural and political contexts for artistic production. Janson, however, contradicted this notion by showing a preference for apolitical art and universal themes, paralleling the postwar democratic model of the apolitical artist. Indicative of the importance of environment to Janson is his concept of exile art in which he discerned a discourse between old and new countries, and, for example, saw traces of two cultures in the art of both Zerbe and Beckmann. His concept of modern art demonstrates his preference for artworks that convey modernism and exile through fragmented images. This is evident in his acquisitions of early twentieth-century cubism and 1930s and 1940s surrealism. At the same time the surrealist works executed either in exile in the U.S. or in the internationally composed French art world of the 1930s also support his international agenda. Yet surrealism's irrationality was certainly seen with skeptical eyes by Janson, who preferred rational aesthetics. Nazi Germany had demonstrated to Janson how irrationalism could be instrumentalized for humanity's worst crimes. In light of the barbaric events in Nazi Europe, Janson's attempts to reclaim the subject's autonomy appear all too idealistic. Perhaps this in part explains why his writings of these years have remained unexamined until now.

I want to thank Keith Holz, Angela Miller and Barbara McCloskey for their valuable comments on early drafts of this essay.

Fig. 32
Karl Zerbe (American, b. Germany, 1903-1972)
Harlequin #1, 1941
Encaustic on canvas, 29 x 39 1/4"
Grey Art Gallery & Study Center, New York
University Art Collection, Gift of Maria Zerbe Norton, 1979
Permission to reproduce granted by Maria Zerbe Norton

CENTENNIAL ADDRESS

H. W. Janson

CENTENNIAL ADDRESS

H. W. Janson

The following address by H. W. Janson was delivered in 1981 on the occasion of the centennial celebration of the Washington University Gallery of Art in St. Louis. Janson's tenure at Washington University, from 1941–1948, included serving as curator, from 1944–1948, of what was then called the Washington University Art Collection. He was instrumental in forming the collection of modern art that is now considered one of the finest university art collections in the country.

Good evening ladies and gentlemen, friends of the Washington University [Gallery of Art] and fellow St. Louisans. We have not lived in St. Louis for, to be exact, thirty-three years, but St. Louis is nevertheless an important part of our lives. Three of our four children were not only conceived but born in St. Louis, so we often have occasion to think back to those strenuous but interesting years. I hope you will not mind if my informal remarks this evening are occasionally tinged with sentiment, because it is not often that one has a chance to return to the place of one's activities as removed by such a historic stretch as thirty-three years from one's present environment and activities.

Of course, the reason why I might be a suitable speaker tonight is the comparatively brief but nevertheless perhaps not insignificant role that I played as curator of the University Art Collection, and some of you may be interested in hearing a little more about the events that transpired between 1945 and 1947. Those are the years during which the contents of what has so kindly been called the Janson room were assembled, and you might like to know how all this was made possible.

Actually, I myself had only very recently reverted to the Department of Art and Archaeology. When this story started, during the war itself, I was teaching physics for the army here on the campus (and that was a tough schedule: twenty-three hours of course contacts a week and no vacations). However, in 1945, I resumed what I considered to be my particular calling. We were just getting used to the idea that the war was over and normal life was slowly returning. To me, normal life meant not only resuming research and teaching in my own field, it also meant that I became aware of the existence of the Washington University Art Collection. I did so by reading certain labels in the City Art Museum [now known as The Saint Louis Art Museum], because attached to certain paintings there were labels saying that they were on loan from the Washington University Art Collection. So I became curious and started wondering, Now, just what is in this art collection? Why is it invisible except when you read it on the labels of certain works of art on display in the City Art Museum?

I found out that there was a great deal to the Washington University Art Collection, but most of it was in storage. For some of it, in fact (as you might know), storage was perhaps not less than what it deserved. When I look back at the things that we decided to sell in the fall of 1945, I visualize shelves and shelves full of beer steins. Somebody had collected beer steins and given the whole collection to the University. Apparently, between 1881 and 1945, there was no screening committee that decided whether a given work of art or collection of artifacts was suitable for a university art collection. Whatever was given was gracefully accepted, so we fell heir not only to this herd of beer steins, but to an equally large collection of English nineteenth-century china. This of course has a certain interest for specialized collectors but little "educational" value, you might say.

Then there were a lot of paintings of varying degrees of merit. While I was familiarizing myself with all these materials, my good friend Charles Nagel, then acting director of the City Art Museum, told me that they were planning to kind of weed out the holdings of the Museum and to quietly, or as quietly as possible, sell off things that they regarded as not wholly desirable—or maybe below the standard that they would like to see among the collections of the City Art Museum. I seized the opportunity and persuaded the University administration that we ought to join into this action and sell the less desirable aspects of the University Art Collection along with the undesirables from the City Art Museum, and thus accumulate a fund from which we might purchase those things that were not at all represented in the collection—namely, twentieth-century art. That is essentially what I accumulated as a result of this sequence of events.

We first of all had to agree on what was to be sold, so a committee was formed to make such a list . . . . Then, when—in a local auction as well as in a New York auction—we found ourselves the happy possessors of $40,000, we made up a list of desiderata.

Those were still the days when the battle for modernism was being fought. It had not yet been won, as it was back in the 1960s. You might say from then on modern art has been so generally accepted that we are now beginning to experience a reevaluation of the things that we despised back in the 1930s and '40s. Some people have asked me, If you had to do it all over again, would you have sold all the things that you sold then?, and I must confess that there are maybe a handful of paintings that I would not include in the sale today, but I still would have sold the Remington [Frederic S. Remington's *A Dash for the Timber* (1889; fig. 33)], which brought the record price of $23,000 at the time. This was such a sensation that it even made *Time* magazine, with a picture of the painting. They evidently thought it was absurd that anyone should pay $23,000 for a painting by Remington. Today, of course, the painting would bring something like a quarter of a million. On the other hand, many of the pictures that we bought with the money from the Remington would now bring not just a quarter of a million, but proba-

Fig. 33
Frederic S. Remington (American, 1861–1909)
A Dash for the Timber, 1889
Oil on canvas, 48¹/₄ x 84¹/₈"
Amon Carter Museum, Fort Worth, Texas
1961.381

bly ten times as much, so that in terms of purely financial gain, one can certainly justify the sale. But quite apart from all that, I never did think of Mr. Remington as a genuine western artist. (My skepticism was borne out when we moved to New York in 1949, because it so happened that we bought a house in New Rochelle, one of the suburbs of New York, practically next door to the Remington "ranch." That is where he lived and that is where he painted his western pictures.) He is still very much in fashion among Oklahoma oil millionaires—that is why his prices have kept up as well as they have—but in terms of the development of twentieth-century art, his significance has not increased over the past thirty years, it seems to me.

I must say that of all the things we were able to buy in 1945 and '46, I am proudest perhaps of Pablo Picasso's *Glass and Bottle of Suze* (1912; cat. no. 16) and Juan Gris' *Still Life with Playing Cards* (*Draughts Board and Playing Cards*) (1916; cat. no. 9) because they are classic works of cubism. The Picasso collage, one of the very earliest in this technique of 1912–13, is called after the label which is taken from the bottle of an aperitif named Suze, and there is in fact a bottle-like shape to which the label is attached. The whole thing is formally a still life, but it is of course not the significance, or even the relationship, of the objects that matters, but the redefinition of pictorial space that makes this such an exciting object to behold. Unfortunately, the strips of the newspaper have of course turned brownish in the course of the years, and no power on earth can possibly bring the original color back, so we have to make certain allowances in retrospect—but on the whole the condition of this Picasso collage is no better and in some respects no worse than that of any other collage of the same age.

Fig. 34
Joseph Stella (American, 1877–1946)
Man in the Elevated (Train), 1918
Oil, wire, and collage on glass,
14 ¹/₄ x 14 ³/₄"
Washington University Gallery of Art,
St. Louis. University purchase, Kende Sale
Fund, 1946

In 1916, another Spaniard, Juan Gris, produced *Still Life with Playing Cards*. This is an oil, and obviously constructed along very much the same lines [as Picasso's *Glass and Bottle of Suze*], but with a kind of austerity and classical precision of form that are only hinted at in the rather more tentative composition of shapes in the Picasso collage. There is, I think, no better painting by Juan Gris anywhere. There are others, two or three perhaps, that I would agree are as good, but none that are better. This is something that one cannot hope to achieve very often, and I will not make such a claim for many of the other things that we bought at the time. After all, we only had $40,000, and while that was quite a heap of money in those years, it was nonetheless a rather limited amount. We would easily have spent it all on one object, or maybe two or three, but what we wanted was to get as many really worthwhile things as the market would permit. I had to stop thinking about anything that cost more than $5,000 because that would have been too large a share of our total capital. You see, most of these things actually cost, well, on the average around $1,000. Some were cheaper; some were more expensive. The most expensive thing, in fact, was the Juan Gris. That's the one object that cost all of $5,000; everything else was less.

The Georges Braque still life [*Nature Morte et Verre* (*Still Life with Glass*) (1930; cat. no. 2)], although it is not a major painting by the artist, is a fully representative example of Braque's version of cubism of the 1920s, and *Man in the Elevated (Train)* (1918; fig. 34) is an equally representative and highly original example by an Italo-American painter–in fact, the only painter then working in America who can be associated with futurism–namely, Joseph Stella. In this context, I think of it also as a still life, but it turns out that the official title of the painting is *Man Riding the Elevated*–that is, the elevated railway in New York, which of course has since been torn down. One looks for the man, and I must confess in a certain difficulty in locating him. The whole thing is a rather complicated construction on glass–that is, in part it is collage applied to glass–a piece of paper from a sort of art catalog that has been carefully clipped out and pasted onto the glass; the rest is simply oil paint painted on the back of the piece of glass to give it a unified shiny surface. Many of the forms are, in fact, separated from each other by carefully laid thin wires to keep the outlines strictly separated and smooth. There is in this picture a kind of dynamism that is a full reflection of the futurist style on the other side of the Atlantic. The painting was done in 1918, so that it was only a few years younger than the older works in this style, and the choice of subject, even though we have difficulty spotting the man in the elevated, is quite typical of futurism, which always prided itself on its willingness–in fact, its determination–to celebrate the dynamism and beauty of modern life, as against the dead past which it officially abominated.

With Theo van Doesburg's *Composition VII: The Three Graces* (1917; cat. no. 20) and Paul Klee's *Überbrückung* (*Transition*) (1935; cat. no. 11) we enter another aspect of twentieth-century art. At first glance they seem to have perhaps more in common than they actually do, because both of them are composed of abstract shapes. The painting by van Doesburg is clearly the more severe of the two, since it consists entirely of rectangles in the primary colors of blue, yellow and red, plus white on a black ground, and also all the forms are arranged along vertical or horizontal axes. That the painting should be called *The Three Graces* must be taken in a metaphorical sense. You have your choice. There are various verticals here that seem to relate to each other. The point, of course, is to strip the artist's language down to its bare essentials. Had we had the money to buy a Mondrian, I would have preferred to, but a van Doesburg was so much cheaper, and almost the same thing for us, that I opted for this picture. It is also, I think, a nice illustration of what one artist may legitimately do that none of his successors can permit themselves to do. A critic once remarked that the first poet to compare the lips of his beloved to a red, red rose was a genius, but the second poet to do so was a goddamned fool. Anyone who would take his lead from paintings like this, and work in this way and in this vocabulary, surely would make a fool of himself. Nevertheless, we here have a classic statement of this extreme formulation that tries to purge art of all elements that do not refer to themselves but to the outside world.

Überbrückung (*Transition*) is by Paul Klee, a very well-known German-Swiss artist, and while the forms here are equally abstract, it has a title that seems to be more in genuine relationship to the forms themselves. There are elements which suggest landscape forms: mountains, maybe a lake [down at the bottom], the sky [up at the top]. There is kind of a transition between elements in the center, so the painting has a kind of drama, a coherence of interlocking shapes that makes the whole thing rather more explicit than any reading you would dare to attempt of the van Doesburg painting.

In the case of Max Ernst, one of the major masters of surrealism, I was particularly lucky. I would not want to claim that *The Eye of Silence* (1943–44; cat. no. 7) is the best Max Ernst there is, but I think it is one of the dozen most important Max Ernst paintings anywhere. Max Ernst at that time was working in this country. He had come over at the very last moment when Europe was falling to the Nazis, and undoubtedly the kind of dream landscape that he creates in this picture had something to do with his experience of the American west–which he loved and in which he traveled extensively. He often implicitly or explicitly referred to these landscape experiences in the west. I remember one painting he did at the time which he entitled *The Colorado de la Meduse*–referring, of course, to *The Raft of the Medusa* (*Le Radeau de la Méduse*, 1819) by Théodore Géricault, but making the Colorado out of the plain radeau. While this is a case of verbal punning, there is a great deal of visual punning going on in this picture called *The Eye of Silence*, in which there is not one eye; there are a good many eyes. It is sort of a collective eye of silence that stares at us. Practically wherever we look there is an eye to respond to ours. Then there are the powerful abstractions in a kind of lake that occupies the lower center of the picture and the great rock structures that seem partially natural, partly sculpted (some of them look like giant petrified octopuses). You can rearrange your imagination as you interpret the painting; it is full of what you might call purposeful ambiguities–that is, ambiguities of a particularly poetic sort. If you simply abandon yourself to whatever responses are evoked in your mind by this painting, you could easily spend hours in front of it. It is a painting of incredible richness.

Another surrealist who is perhaps as important in his own way as Max Ernst (although his work does not have the interpretive richness and variety of Ernst) is Yves Tanguy, who always imagined some endless atmospheric plane, as he does in *La Tour Marine* (*Tower of the Sea*) (1944; cat. no. 19). Here a plane sort of recedes into infinity and is populated at intervals with these monuments, these structures, that are very precisely defined in three-dimensional terms. The light, too, is a very precise light, almost like the light on the moon, but there is no atmosphere to soften the blackness of the shadows. If you look at a form you can see the shadow is as clear, as precise, as substantial as the form itself. Here again, I do not want to claim that this is the best Yves Tanguy there is. There are larger and more ambitious works, but it is a very beautiful example of Yves Tanguy's work.

The third major surrealist that I wanted very badly to have in the collection is yet another Spaniard, Joan Miró. Here I was very fortunate indeed. I would say that *Peinture* (*Painting*) (1933; cat. no. 15) is the second-best Miró–the best being the companion to this painting, which is in the Museum of Modern Art and is a tiny bit better than this one. But I think this is a classic statement of what Miró had to say when he was at his richest and his most harmonious, both in terms of color and in terms of these biomorphic shapes which appear to contract and expand as you look at them.

Of course, the collection, we felt, could not be limited to the great Europeans; it should also include younger artists, especially younger artists from the new world, and there are two examples. One is a still life by William Baziotes (*Still Life* [1945; fig. 35]), who was just coming into prominence and who has since then more than fulfilled his promise, I believe. (The collection has since acquired another later picture by the same artist, *Night Form* [1947]). The other is *Lion and Horse* (1942; fig. 36), a work by what

I consider the most impressive living Mexican painter, Rufino Tamayo, who often works with sort of primeval experiences. The subject here actually has a very long history: lions have been attacking horses in painting and sculpture ever since ancient Roman times, but rarely has it been done with the kind of force that you see in a painting like this. Here, especially in his choice of colors, which has really no counterpart anywhere else, some quintessential Mexican quality seems to me to come through that makes this painting an important one to own and to contemplate.

Then there is yet another aspect of twentieth-century art that had to be represented in our collection—what you might call the expressionist aspect, to which *Les Artistes mit Gemüse* (*Artists with Vegetable*), or *Four Men Around a Table* (1943; cat. no. 1) by Max Beckmann very clearly belongs. It

Fig. 35
William A. Baziotes (American, 1912–1964)
Still Life, 1945
Oil on canvas, 36¹/₄ x 47¹⁵/₁₆"
Washington University Gallery of Art,
St. Louis. University purchase, Kende Sale
Fund, 1946

Fig. 36
Rufino Tamayo (Mexican, 1899–1991)
Lion and Horse, 1942
Oil on canvas, 36¹/₃ x 46¹/₂"
Washington University Gallery of Art,
St. Louis. University purchase, Kende Sale
Fund, 1946
© State of the artist in support of Fundación Olga
y Rufino Tamayo, A.C.

Fig. 37
Philip Guston (American, 1913–1980)
If This Be Not I, 1945
Oil on canvas, 42¹/₄ x 55¹/₄"
Washington University Gallery of Art,
St. Louis. University purchase, Kende Sale
Fund, 1946
Permission to reproduce granted by McKee Gallery

is a self-portrait with friends, painted just two years earlier [than when Washington University acquired it], while Beckmann was still leading a sort of underground existence in the Netherlands during the war. *If This Be Not I* (1945; fig. 37) is by Philip Guston, who at that time was actually teaching at the Washington University School of Art. Its style is transitional in the very curious development that the work of Guston has undergone. He died only very recently. I must confess that I don't understand his most recent phase, yet in a painting like *If This Be Not I*, he is clearly trying to work with the socially conscious vocabulary of the WPA era–but to broaden it into a kind of general poetic sensibility that says something about the human condition without attaching it to a specific set of social circumstances. So the painting is full of these–you might call them neurotic or you might call them poetic–ideas that have somehow been shaped into a rather complicated kind of universe. One might have similar thoughts about the symbolic aspect of the four friends in Beckmann's *Les Artistes mit Gemüse*, each of whom has an attribute: a fish; a great big root vegetable (a sort of giant carrot–the kind of root vegetable that people had to live on in Holland when there was a near starvation condition at the end of the war); Beckmann himself has a mirror; and the fourth man has something which I am not quite sure what it is, but it was also undoubtedly meant to be a meaningful subject. And the four friends are related in a way that goes beyond the accident of their being together or the accident of their friendship.

We also wanted some sculpture, and the few pieces of sculpture that I was able to buy constitute perhaps a broader range of the possibilities of that medium than is demonstrated by the paintings. One of these pieces is the Sepik River, New Guinea wood carving [*Homme Oiseau (Man-Bird)*] (c. 1900; fig. 38)]. I did not buy it from a dealer in "primitive" art; I bought it from the Pierre Matisse Gallery in New York, a gallery run by one of the sons of the painter Henri Matisse and long-established as one of the chief dealers in twentieth-century art. He had this piece because he had fallen in love with it many years earlier, and I had a hard time persuading him to part with it, although it turned out not to be terribly expensive. It is, I think, the best piece of New Guinea sculpture in any American museum, and quite unforgettable in the way in which the spirit of the dead here suddenly takes off soaringly in the shape of a bird that grows from the head of this ancestral figure.

Reclining Figure (1933; fig. 39) shows a reclining woman by Henry Moore, who, of course, had established his prominence in the 1930s as an English experimental sculptor of extraordinary daring and precision. I liked this particular piece as against others that were available at the time because it was Moore's first piece in reinforced concrete; he was trying a new medium. The Washington University Art Collection has had a good deal of trouble with this piece from a purely material point of view; it is apt to be damaged. It was, in fact, damaged a couple of times when it was out on loan. There are certain built-in instabilities here that make it somewhat of a trial to own, but just because it is the first of its kind

Fig. 38
Homme Oiseau (Man-Bird), c. 1900
Sepik River, New Guinea
Carved polychrome wood, 48 x 43³/₄"
Washington University Gallery of Art,
St. Louis, University purchase, Kende Sale
Fund, 1946

Fig. 39
Henry Moore (British, 1898–1986)
Reclining Figure, 1933
Reinforced carved concrete,
17 x 30³/₄ x 12¹⁵/₁₆"
Washington University Gallery of Art,
St. Louis, University purchase, Kende Sale
Fund, 1946
Reproduced by permission of the Henry Moore
Foundation

Fig. 40
Antoine Pevsner (French, b. Russia,
1886–1962)
Bas Relief en Creux (Sunken Bas Relief),
1926–27
Relief in brass and bronze,
23⁵/₁₆ x 24⁵/₁₆ x 13⅛"
Washington University Gallery of Art,
St. Louis, University purchase, Kende Sale
Fund, 1946
© 2002 Artists Rights Society (ARS),
New York/ADAGP, Paris

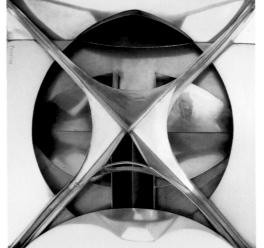

A third piece of sculpture, which is very different indeed from the other two, illustrates yet another possibility. *Bas Relief en Creux (Sunken Bas Relief)* (1926–27; fig. 40) is a constructivist work by Antoine Pevsner, a Russian and the brother of Naum Gabo, whose name is perhaps even better known as a master for things of this kind. This is a work that you can look at while it is either hanging on a wall or

it is a kind of landmark in the history of modern sculpture, and that's why I felt very lucky that we were able to get it.

lying on a table, and I've never been able to make up my mind which is the more appropriate way of looking at it. One might interpret it, if one wishes, as the model for some architectural fantasy—some very elaborate version that goes beyond the famous St. Louis Arch in the boldness of its architectural imagination, but it remains here on a small scale. Obviously, it is a splendid display for the equivalent of solids and hollows which work against each other, into each other, in a great variety of ways, and the highly polished material—brass—brings out these qualities in a rather memorable fashion.

I'd like to say, in conclusion, a few things about other experiences I have had with university art galleries and about the function that I think university art galleries ought to have in the context of a college or university. Some of the university or college art museums that exist today can look back on a history even older than that of the Washington University Art Collection, although one hundred years is a very respectable record indeed. Back in 1881, I think, you could have counted the number of institutions of higher learning that had an art collection on the fingers of one (possibly mutilated) hand. Since then, of course, they have grown apace, but there are still a good many campuses where the real importance of such a collection as an educational resource is not fully appreciated. I've always regarded one aspect of whatever missionary work I can do in my field not only is to advocate the establishment of the university art collection where none exists now, but to plot out its educational value and to address how it really ought to be used. It is difficult to lay down the law in this respect because that depends very much on the local situation, on the local resources—whether there are important art collectors and important art public in the area, which in a small college town very often is not the case, unlike in major cities like St. Louis and New York.

New York University, you'll be glad to note, also has an art collection that is considerably younger than Washington University. New York University at one point was offered the [A. E.] Gallatin collection of modern art, known at that time as the Museum of Living Art. And as late as 1940 (that was before I came to New York University), no one was a sufficiently strong advocate of modern art to persuade the administration that this was an invaluable collection, so Mr. Gallatin finally took the whole thing away from the University and gave it to the Philadelphia Museum [of Art], where it is conspicuously on display to this very day.

Some fifteen years later, some people at New York University, including myself, felt that something ought to be done to expiate this colossal sin of omission and indifference, and we have since built not only an art collection but also a university art gallery which is flourishing and which the administration is now beginning to realize is a major source of favorable public relations. It has practically no competition around Washington Square, where it is located. The Whitney Museum of American Art once used to be on Eighth Street, but since it moved uptown there is really nothing of this sort in our area. The Grey Art

Gallery, named after the kindly old lady who helped us establish the Gallery, represents not only an important enrichment of the neighborhood, but to an even greater extent an educational enrichment for a whole variety of students–not only students in the Department of Fine Arts, but students in Education, and of course the entire undergraduate community–who have a chance to study works of art at close range such as they would not have in a museum–especially not in New York, where every museum is so conscious of the importance of packing in numbers that you often simply cannot get even close to the works of art.

In contrast with that, the university art gallery provides an environment where you can really confront a work without facing the competition of thousands who want to do exactly the same thing at exactly the same moment. If you take courses in the history of art, then you should be given the opportunity to actually handle the works in a seminar room. You should have a chance to really become acquainted with the work of art as a physical object. You should learn how one can tell a genuine Rembrandt etching from even the most masterful imitation of such an etching, and you should learn that such imitations exist that are so good they are printed only on paper with a special watermark (which, of course, cannot be eliminated, otherwise the world would be fooled by reproductions of Rembrandt etchings that are to all but the most experienced eye indistinguishable from the original). This does not mean that it is not important to distinguish the two: it makes it doubly important to tell which is the real McCoy and which is only an approximation. It is experiences of this sort that can mark a student for life: suddenly something awakens in him when he handles an object that cannot be awakened in any other way.

So let me conclude by wishing the Washington University Art Collection a happy second hundred years. I will not be around to help you celebrate at the end of that period, but at least my good wishes are with you.

This address has been edited for brevity and to fit the print format. It was transcribed by M. Todd Hignite and Ivana Salander, 2000–2001.

CATALOG

Bradley Fratello and George V. Speer

MAX BECKMANN
(German, 1884–1950)

1

Les Artistes mit Gemüse (Artists with Vegetable), or **Four Men Around a Table,** 1943
Oil on canvas, 58 ¹⁵/₁₆ x 45 ³/₁₆"
University purchase, Kende Sale Fund, 1946

Provenance

	Artist
–1946	Buchholz Gallery (New York, NY)
1946–	Washington University Gallery of Art (St. Louis, MO)

When Max Beckmann's work was shown in the United States after World War II, his reputation as an historically important figure in German modernism was augmented by his credentials as a refugee from Adolf Hitler and a "violent anti-Nazi."[1] In remarks published after the artist's death, for example, Perry T. Rathbone of the City Art Museum (now The Saint Louis Art Museum) recalled the artist's "fascist denunciation, exile and . . . life underground."[2] In Les Artistes mit Gemüse, the image of the artist sustaining the life of the spirit in a time of war thus accorded well with Beckmann's public persona at the time in which the work was acquired.[3] This self-constructed myth of the artist as keeper of the faith was sustained by no less influential a figure than Alfred H. Barr, Jr., of the Museum of Modern Art. Barr singled Beckmann out as an example of the ideal artist who perseveres towards "freedom, perfection and truth" in the face of totalitarian ideologies.[4] Yet, although Beckmann believed—as did Barr—that art should be an autonomous and transcendent sphere of experience outside of political realities, the actual circumstances under which this work was created point to the impossibility of that belief.[5] In exile in Amsterdam from 1937 to 1945, Beckmann enjoyed privileges offered by highly-placed Nazi officials and wealthy Germans, who purchased his works for secret shipment out of Holland, warned of imminent confiscations, and provided the artist with funds for the duration of the war.[6] Perhaps in recognition of the hard moral choices that the artist had been obliged to make, Rathbone—the artist's good friend and sponsor in St. Louis—asserted in his eulogy that "[In his] concern with good and evil, with beauty and ugliness lay Max Beckmann's philosophy of life; . . . neither could be excluded."[7] [GS]

1. Art Digest 20, no. 15 (May 1, 1946): p. 13.
2. Perry T. Rathbone, cited in Erhard Göpel, In Memoriam: Max Beckmann, 12.2.1884–27.12.1950 (West Germany: Max-Beckmann-Gesellschaft, 1953), p. 9.
3. See Barbara Buenger, "Antifascism or Autonomous Art?," in Exiles and Emigrés: The Flight of European Artists from Hitler, ed. Stephanie Barron and Sabine Eckmann (Los Angeles and New York: Los Angeles County Museum of Art and Harry N. Abrams, 1997), pp. 58–62.
4. Alfred H. Barr, Jr., What Is Modern Painting? (New York: Museum of Modern Art and Simon & Schuster, 1946), pp. 25, 43–44.
5. Max Beckmann, On My Painting (New York: Buchholz Gallery & Curt Valentin, 1941), pp. 3–4.
6. Buenger, "Antifascism or Autonomous Art?," pp. 58, 61; see also Lynn H. Nicholas, The Rape of Europa: The Fate of Europe's Treasures in the Third Reich and the Second World War (New York: Alfred A. Knopf, 1994), pp. 81–114.
7. Rathbone, cited in Göpel, Max Beckmann, p. 9.

GEORGES BRAQUE
(French, 1882–1963)

2

Nature Morte et Verre (Still Life with Glass), 1930
Oil on canvas, 20³/₁₆ x 25⁵/₈"
University purchase, Kende Sale Fund, 1946

Provenance

	Artist
–1946	Paul Rosenberg and Co. (New York, NY)
1946–	Washington University Gallery of Art (St. Louis, MO)

"One should, I think, regard Braque as being first and foremost an exponent of still-life, for not only are the great majority of his pictures still-lifes, but in their delineation he has made himself pre-eminent among his contemporaries. It is these pictures which have given him the wide reputation he enjoys."[1] A. E. Gallatin's assessment of Georges Braque's work, published in 1943, was among the most recent English language publications about the artist when *Nature Morte et Verre*, an exemplar of the genre, entered the collection of Washington University. It was the first work by Braque that the University owned, and the only painted example of cubism by either him or Pablo Picasso in the collection at the time.

Cubism had come into its own in the United States in 1936, when the Museum of Modern Art staged the exhibition *Cubism and Abstract Art*. As one of the style's pioneers, along with Picasso, Braque held an important place in the history of twentieth-century painting, and even such a relatively late example of cubism as *Nature Morte et Verre* had already received wide publication and exhibition throughout Europe.[2] Acquired directly from Braque by Paul Rosenberg of Paris in 1930, the painting traveled extensively in Scandinavia, Switzerland, London, and Zurich in the 1930s. Rosenberg hosted a Parisian exhibition of Braque's work that featured the painting in 1940 before his collection was looted by the Nazis and he was forced to emigrate.[3] *Nature Morte et Verre* was one of the works Rosenberg was able to bring with him to the United States. Among his earliest exhibitions in New York was a Braque exhibition and an exhibition featuring Picasso and Braque, both in 1943. The year appears to have been a high-water mark for Braque's notoriety in the United States, when books and exhibitions celebrating cubism were popular both in the United States and abroad. [BF]

1. A. E. Gallatin, *Georges Braque* (New York: Wittenborn and Company, 1943), unpaginated.
2. See for example *G. Braque*, exh. cat. (Basel: Kunstmuseum, 1933), cat. no. 152, and Carl Einstein, *Georges Braque* (Paris: Editions des Chroniques du Jour, 1934), plate LXXXIII.
3. With the help of influential American supporters such as the St. Louis City Art Museum's president Louis La Beaume, Rosenberg fled to New York where he soon established a gallery on 72nd Street. (See Rosenberg to La Beaume, September 27, 1940. The Saint Louis Art Museum archives.)

ALEXANDER CALDER
(American, 1898–1976)

3

Bayonets Menacing a Flower, 1945
Painted sheet metal and wire, 45 x 51 x 18 ½"
University purchase, McMillan Fund, 1946

Provenance

	Artist
–1946	Buchholz Gallery (New York, NY)
1946–	Washington University Gallery of Art (St. Louis, MO)

When *Bayonets Menacing a Flower* was acquired in 1946, critic Reed Hynds cited the scarcity of important American art in the Washington University Gallery of Art while celebrating the introduction of modern European works into the collection.[1] In fact, Alexander Calder's sculpture would seem to have offered the best of both worlds, for its gestural freedom in three dimensions evokes the confidence of postwar American painting as well as the imaginative vocabulary of the Europeans who had helped to shape Calder's career. Criticism of Calder in the American art press of the 1940s expressed a certain ambivalence towards the surrealist elements in his work. A review of a joint exhibition with Yves Tanguy in 1943 acknowledged a shared language of form between the two artists, yet drew a subtle but important distinction by using the term "objects in space" to refer to Calder's creations, as opposed to "spatial fantasies" for Tanguy's.[2] In the same year, a retrospective associated Calder's organic abstractions with those of Joan Miró, Paul Klee, and other more lighthearted surrealists, while denying the existence of "unhappy thoughts, lurking" or of "subconscious broodings given form."[3] A common strategy in American criticism of this period was to make such distinctions between a "darker" European imagination and a healthier, more optimistic American sensibility. Perhaps as a reaction to the war, Calder's critics emphasized the gentleness of his pieces as well as characteristics of humor, vigor, and a spirit of scientific inquiry in his work. Calder was also differentiated from the mythology surrounding the abstract expressionists, who were often regarded as tainted with European introspection. Because he was seen to balance the bravado of the New York School with mechanical aptitude and objectivity, Calder in the postwar period appeared to reflect "the essential" genius of America–its capacity to make things work."[4]

[GS]

1. Reed Hynds, "Yielding Place to New," *Art News* 45, no. 4 (June 1946): pp. 62–63.

2. *Art Digest* 17, no. 17 (June 1943): p. 12.

3. *Art Digest* 18, no. 1 (October 1943): p. 6.

4. Ibid. The writer speaks of Calder's "American vernacular." See also "The Passing Shows," *Art News* 44, no. 15 (November 1945): p. 26; Douglas Cooper, "The Literature of Art," *Burlington Magazine* 87 (1945): p. 224; and David Sylvester, review of "The Venice Biennale," *The Nation* 171, no. 11 (September 1950): pp. 232–33.

WILLEM DE KOONING
(American, b. Holland, 1904–1997)

4
Saturday Night, 1956
Oil on canvas, 68³/₄ x 79"
University purchase, Bixby Fund, 1956

Provenance

		Artist
	1956	Sidney Janis Gallery (New York, NY)
	1956–	Washington University Gallery of Art

When *Saturday Night* was acquired by the Washington University Gallery of Art, Willem de Kooning had recently returned to a greater degree of abstraction after years of controversial figural work. The crucial question seems to have been whether this less-representational idiom constituted progress or fatigue on the artist's part. *Saturday Night* was singled out in two reviews that articulated this debate. Dore Ashton offered an assessment of de Kooning's career that was both admiring and eulogistic. On the one hand, the artist's standing as a "charismatic chieftain" of abstract expressionism was only underscored by the technical mastery displayed in this painting, but the "breathtaking boldnesses, scintillating witticisms [and] shocking negligences" were seen to lack the emotional authenticity of the *Woman* series. De Kooning's gestures were "thoughtlessly" proffered as "mannerisms," which Ashton attributed to the strain on the artist of being an iconic example to a new generation of painters.[1] Implicit in Ashton's critique is the twofold awareness that the triumph of de Kooning's generation was history, and that a very different idiom was emerging in the work of Jasper Johns, Robert Rauschenberg, and others who appropriated and ironized the pictorial rhetoric of abstract expressionism. Thomas Hess, who wrote a monograph on de Kooning less than three years later, published a hyperbolic, defensive reiteration of this rhetoric, asserting that the "brutal drive to master the material" evident in *Saturday Night* offered "a sense of rawness … like an introduction to a new race of people" and predicted that de Kooning would "replace Picasso and Miró as the most influential painter at work today."[2] Both critics addressed, however obliquely, the realization that a moment in the arc of modernism had passed, and that the bad boys of the New York School had aged into *eminences grises*. [GS]

1. Dore Ashton, "Art," *Arts & Architecture* 73 (June 1956): p. 10. See also her comments of only six months earlier regarding the "apogee of abstract power" in the *Woman* series, in "Art," *Arts & Architecture* 72 (December 1955): pp. 33–34.
2. Thomas B. Hess, "Selecting from the Flow of Spring Shows," *Art News* 55, no. 2 (April 1956): pp. 25, 100.

JEAN DUBUFFET
(French, 1901–1985)

5

Poches aux Yeux (Bags Under the Eyes), 1959
Paper mâché, 18 ⁵/₈ x 7 ¹/₁₆ x 3 ½"
Gift of Florence S. Weil, 1982

Provenance

	Artist
–1962	James Wise (Collonge Bellerive, Switzerland)
	World House Galleries (New York, NY)
1962–82	Collection Florence S. Weil (St. Louis, MO)
1982–	Washington University Gallery of Art (St. Louis, MO)

6

Tête Barbue (Bearded Head), 1959
Driftwood with barnacles, 11 ¹/₈ x ¹/₈ x 4"
Gift of Florence S. Weil, 1982

Provenance

	Artist
–1962	Galerie Berggruen (Paris, France)
	World House Galleries (New York, NY)
1962–82	Collection Florence S. Weil (St. Louis, MO)
1982–	Washington University Gallery of Art (St. Louis, MO)

Mr. and Mrs. Richard K. Weil, St. Louis collectors and benefactors of the Washington University Gallery of Art, acquired *Poches aux Yeux* and *Tête Barbue* as a pair from New York's World House Galleries in November 1962. The two works remained a pair when donated in 1982. *Tête Barbue*, however, unlike *Poches aux Yeux*, had been exhibited twice in the three years since its "completion." This *objet trouvé* had found a place in a retrospective of Jean Dubuffet's work at the World House Galleries in 1960, whose catalog illustrated it, and at a Dubuffet retrospective at the Museum of Modern Art (MOMA) earlier in the year the Weils purchased it. *Poches aux Yeux*, while not a found object, shares the raw, unmediated quality of its companion, and visually unifies the pair in a manner that corresponds to their similar provenances.

Peter Selz, curator of the MOMA show, had organized an exhibition there in 1959 titled *New Images of Man*, which included several of Dubuffet's painted and assembled *Barbes*, or bearded figures, of which the Washington University piece is not usually, but could be considered, a part. In the *New Images* catalog, Dubuffet wrote: "I have liked to carry the human image on to a plane of seriousness where the futile embellishments of aesthetics no longer have any place."[1] The statement privileges the unworked, discovered quality so important to *Tête Barbue* and renders the work even more relevant to Dubuffet's series, already celebrated in the early 1960s. The Pierre Matisse Gallery, from which the Weils purchased Joan Miró's *Peinture* (1925; cat. no. 14) in 1959, had held a Dubuffet retrospective that year, possibly fueling the Weils' interest in the French artist. The introduction to the catalog for this retrospective had characterized Dubuffet's work since 1944 as "the painter plunged into the search for new 'materials,'" an immersion that "a great number of painters did not wait long to borrow … from him," thus situating him at the forefront of recent art developments.[2] [BF]

1. Jean Dubuffet, in *New Images of Man*, exh. cat. (New York: Museum of Modern Art, 1959), p. 13.
2. Georges Limbour, "Jean Dubuffet," in *Jean Dubuffet*, exh. cat. (New York: Pierre Matisse Gallery, 1959), unpaginated.

MAX ERNST
(German, 1891–1976)

7

The Eye of Silence, 1943–44
Oil on canvas, 43¼ x 56¼"
University purchase, Kende Sale Fund, 1946
© 2001 Artists Rights Society (ARS), New York/ADAGP, Paris

Provenance

	Artist
–1946	Julien Levy Gallery (New York, NY)
1946–	Washington University Gallery of Art (St. Louis, MO)

For Reed Hynds, Max Ernst's *The Eye of Silence* and Yves Tanguy's *La Tour Marine* (1944; cat. no. 19) typified the startlingly modern art that might well have the "good burghers" of St. Louis "turning in their graves."[1] The critic's humorous but encouraging review of the University's new acquisitions suggests the difficulties faced by the Europeans in exile in the United States. Ernst's struggle for recognition in this country was due in part to a widespread perception of surrealism as the product of a corrupt and effete European culture. A typical reaction characterized his work as "unhealthy" and offering "a fetid harvest of abnormal creatures."[2] But surrealism was particularly suspect in the context of a carefully circumscribed idea of modern art then emerging, one which delimited painting as strictly self-referential, concerned only with questions of line, color, and form. Writing in 1944, Clement Greenberg–the chief theorist of the "new" modernism–placed Ernst in a particular group of painters whom he thought to have betrayed the true promise of surrealism. Whereas Joan Miró, Jean Arp, and André Masson "surrendered to the medium" in their practice of automatic drawing, and in so doing furthered the discipline of modern painting, the illusionistic imagery of Ernst, Yves Tanguy, and Salvador Dalí was not art at all, but "literature." Their work brought modern art down to the taste of the public instead of raising that taste to a higher level, and, according to Greenberg, was entirely too symptomatic of the self-conscious decadence and "sense of chic" among the exiles and their American sponsors. Ernst's variant of surrealism was considered to be of the same kitsch value as "calendar reproduction, postal card, chromeotype, and magazine illustration."[3] [GS]

1. Reed Hynds, "Yielding Place to New," *Art News* 45, no. 4 (June 1946): p. 63.
2. Eleanor Jewett, "Art Institute's Surrealism Show Opens June 29," *Chicago Sunday Tribune*, May 31, 1942, p. 4.
3. Clement Greenberg, "Surrealist Painting," *The Nation* 159, nos. 7, 8 (August 12 and 19, 1944): pp. 192–93; 219–20.

ARSHILE GORKY
(American, b. Armenia, 1904–1948)

8

Golden Brown, 1943–44
Oil on canvas, 43 ¹³⁄₁₆ x 55 ⁹⁄₁₆"
University purchase, Bixby Fund, 1953

Provenance

	Artist's estate
–1953	Sidney Janis Gallery (New York, NY)
1953–	Washington University Gallery of Art (St. Louis, MO)

When *Golden Brown* was purchased in 1953, Arshile Gorky's reputation had been fiercely debated since his death in 1948. Critics argued the formal achievements in Gorky's work as well as the value of his personal and thematic mythologies. These responses reflected the artist's own refusal in the 1940s to ally himself entirely with André Breton's surrealists or with the young Turks of New York. Some writers were suspicious of a "process of apotheosis" in which the artist–who appeared to them to be derivative in his style and undisciplined in his practice–seemed merely the newest "darling of the dilettantes," the latest trophy name after Salvador Dalí, Paul Klee, and Jackson Pollock.[1] Gorky's supporters aligned his career with those of Pollock and Willem de Kooning, celebrating his larger-than-life persona as well as his technical achievement in "orchestrating the full Byzantine splendor of which his Armenian temperament was capable."[2] Clement Greenberg made a common comparison between Gorky and Joan Miró in referring to Gorky as "second to no painter of our time in sheer finesse."[3] This opinion was disputed by the English critic David Sylvester, who felt that Gorky was among a group of "ham-fisted" and "frenetic" American abstractionists.[4] Greenberg's estimation of Gorky ignored the artist's personal mythology, however, in favor of questions of technique; to state that Gorky's line and color were indebted to Miró was to place him in the company of a particular group of surrealists who, in Greenberg's opinion, anticipated the modernist discipline of "surrender to the medium" through their use of automatic gesture.[5] In this sense, Gorky's achievement, like that of Greenberg's other heroes in the New York School, was to carry the European tradition to its inevitable "triumph" in the United States. [GS]

1. Emily Genauer in the *New York Herald Tribune* and Howard Devree in the *New York Times* as cited in "Gorky: Was He Tops or Second Rate?," *Art Digest* 25, no. 8 (January 15, 1951): pp. 9, 30. See also James Fitzsimmons, "The Late Gorky," *Art Digest* 27, no. 11 (March 1, 1953): p. 16; and James Thrall Soby, who noted that "legends [of] artists … are of interest only so long as they are sustained by adequate creative gifts," in "Arshile Gorky," *Magazine of Art* 44, no. 2 (February 1951): p. 56.

2. Elaine de Kooning, "Gorky: Painter of his Own Legend," in *Art News* 49, no. 9 (January 1951): p. 39. See also Louise Ballard, "Art," *Arts & Architecture* 68 (May 1951): p. 10.

3. Clement Greenberg, "The European View of American Art," *The Nation* 171, no. 22 (November 25, 1950): pp. 490–92.

4. David Sylvester, "Mr. Sylvester Replies," ibid., pp. 492–93. See also Sylvester, "The Venice Biennale," *The Nation* 171, no. 11 (September 9, 1950): pp. 232–33. This debate was essentially one of nationalist prejudices, filled with accusations of "blindness" and "condescension."

5. Greenberg, "Surrealist Painting," *The Nation* 159, nos. 7, 8 (August 12 and 19, 1944): pp. 192–93; 219–20.

JUAN GRIS
(Spanish, 1887–1927)

9

Still Life with Playing Cards
(*Draughts Board and Playing Cards*), 1916
Oil on canvas, 28 7/8 x 23 3/4"
University purchase, Kende Sale Fund, 1946

Provenance

	Artist
1929	Leonce Rosenberg (Paris, France)
	Charles Daniel (New York, NY)
1934	Alanson Hartpence (New York, NY)
	Perls Galleries (New York, NY)
1944	Buchholz Gallery (New York, NY)
–1946	Vladimir Golschmann (St. Louis, MO)
1946	Theodore Schempp
1946–	Washington University Gallery of Art (St. Louis, MO)

Still Life with Playing Cards stood as one of Juan Gris' most recognizable images in the United States in the mid-1940s, when H. W. Janson purchased it with funds raised through the Kende sale. A review in *Art News* of an important Gris retrospective at the Buchholz Gallery in New York chose this painting for illustration, thus designating it as a signature example of what the author called the artist's "lyrical cubism."[1] The painting represented the midpoint, according to the article, of Gris' strongest period: "the work of 1914–1918 seems superior, and shows his easy, skillful handling of planes, his tightly knit compositions, and the wonderful flow of linear obbligato throughout the whole."[2]

Purchased from Theodore Schempp, along with Paul Klee's *Überbrückung* (1935; cat. no. 11), *Still Life with Playing Cards* was the most expensive item acquired through the Kende sale. Noting the high cost of the painting twice, critic Reed Hynds also chose to illustrate this work in his tribute to the Gallery of Art's new acquisitions in *Art News*, selecting it over works by Pablo Picasso, Fernand Léger, Paul Klee, Joan Miró, and William Baziotes.[3] It could thus be considered the centerpiece of Janson's campaign to establish Washington University as a prominent collector of twentieth-century modernism.

[BF]

1. Aline B. Louchheim, "Looking Back at Gris, Lyrical Cubist," *Art News* 43, no. 5 (April 1944): p. 23.
2. Ibid.
3. Reed Hynds, "Yielding Place to New," *Art News* 45, no. 4 (June 1946): pp. 32, 63.

MARSDEN HARTLEY
(American, 1877–1943)

10

The Iron Cross, 1915
Oil on canvas, 47⅝ x 47⅝"
University purchase, Bixby Fund, 1952

Provenance

Artist

–1952   Paul Rosenberg & Co. (New York, NY)

1952–   Washington University Gallery of Art
         (St. Louis, MO)

When critic Reed Hynds remarked in an article in *Art News* on Washington University's acquisitions of the mid-1940s that "the University's collection is most deficient in American works," he also noted "it is expected that this lack will be remedied chiefly through the Bixby Fund, which provides a substantial amount annually for the acquisition of American works."[1] Over the next several years the Bixby Fund did exactly that. Works by Stuart Davis, Arthur Dove, and Jimmy Ernst joined Marsden Hartley's *The Iron Cross* in bolstering Washington University's American modernist holdings in 1952 alone.

The Iron Cross had been a centerpiece for the Brooklyn Museum of Art's exhibition *Revolution and Tradition* the year before the University purchased it from Paul Rosenberg; it appeared on the cover of the Museum's *Bulletin* to commemorate the show.[2] John I. H. Baur curated the exhibition and published Hartley's German Officer series, of which *The Iron Cross* is a key work. He ascribed central importance to *Revolution and Tradition in Modern American Art* the same year. He ascribed central importance to Hartley's German Officer series, of which *The Iron Cross* is a key work. "[It] was Marsden Hartley who made the most personal use of German expressionism in an imposing group of roughly painted, free-form abstractions done between 1913 and 1915. Heavy and rhythmical, with richly modulated color, they are among the most original paintings of their kind by an American in these years."[3] Hartley's German Officer paintings combine European style and a distinctly American sensibility, giving the works both cosmopolitan and nationalistic value. Baur did not note their importance as Hartley's ode to a lost lover–the soldier Karl von Freiburg, whose initials appear elsewhere in the series–but restricted his assessment of the works to a modernist paradigm. [BF]

1. Reed Hynds, "Yielding Place to New," *Art News* 45, no. 4 (June 1946): pp. 62–63.

2. *Brooklyn Museum Bulletin* 13, no. 1 (1951): cover.

3. John I. H. Baur, *Revolution and Tradition in Modern American Art* (Cambridge, MA: Harvard University Press, 1951), p. 53

PAUL KLEE
(Swiss, 1879–1940)

11
Überbrückung (Transition), 1935
Oil on canvas, 17 x 25 3/4"
University purchase, Kende Sale Fund, 1945

© 2002 Artists Rights Society (ARS), New York/VG Bild-Kunst, Bonn

Provenance

	Artist
–1945	Nierendorf Gallery (New York, NY)
1945	Theodore Schempp
1945–	Washington University Gallery of Art

Dozens of monographs and retrospective exhibitions, both American and European, of the work of Paul Klee appeared in the five years after his death in 1940. An exhibition curated by the Museum of Modern Art's Alfred H. Barr, Jr. was among the most important of the American shows, traveling throughout the United States and including a stop at the City Art Museum of St. Louis (now The Saint Louis Art Museum). Barr's praise of Klee situated him among the most important artists of the century: he claimed that "not even Picasso approach[ed] him in sheer inventiveness."[1]

Überbrückung was not exhibited in Klee's lifetime or in the five years before it entered the Washington University collection. It belonged to Karl Nierendorf, whose important collection of Klee's works enriched the Museum of Modern Art's exhibition before passing to Theodore Schempp, from whom H. W. Janson purchased both it and Juan Gris' *Still Life with Playing Cards* (1916; cat. no. 9) with funds from the Kende sale. Recommending *Überbrückung,* along with Joan Miró's *Peinture* (1933; cat. no 15), to Chancellor Arthur Compton for purchase on Janson's advice, Lawrence Hill called Klee "one of the most important and influential post-Cubist painters" and referred to the painting as "an excellent and moderately priced specimen of the master's work."[2] The work's relative obscurity, coupled with Klee's fast-rising (if posthumous) star in the art world, made *Überbrückung* a strategic acquisition. Hill urged decisiveness on the part of the University: "it is particularly advisable to purchase a work by Paul Klee now, since his work is apt to be much more expensive in the future."[3] [BF]

1. Alfred H. Barr, Jr., "Introduction," *Paul Klee,* exh. cat. (New York: Museum of Modern Art, 1940), p. 6.
2. Lawrence Hill to Arthur H. Compton, November 12, 1945, Washington University Gallery of Art archives.
3. Ibid.

JACQUES LIPCHITZ
(American, b. Lithuania, 1891–1973)

12

Pierrot with Clarinet, 1919

Bronze, 29 3/4 x 8 13/16 x 10 1/16"

Gift of Mr. and Mrs. Richard K. Weil, 1978

© Estate of Jacques Lipchitz, courtesy Marlborough Gallery, New York

Provenance

	Artist
–1956	Otto Gerson Gallery (New York, NY)
1956–78	Mr. and Mrs. Richard K. Weil (St. Louis, MO)
1978–	Washington University Gallery of Art (St. Louis, MO)

Pierrot with Clarinet, although the third sculpture by Jacques Lipchitz to enter the Washington University collection, was and remains today the Gallery of Art's only example of Lipchitz's cubist-inspired work from the 1910s. In his letter of 1978 recognizing its gift by Mr. and Mrs. Richard K. Weil family, then-director Gerald Bolas, instead of comparing this sculpture to the Gallery of Art's other works by Lipchitz (*Joy of Orpheus* [1946] and *Mother and Child* [1941–45]), noted that *Pierrot with Clarinet* was "an exceptionally complimentary addition to our holdings of cubist-related work of the teens. The juxtaposition ... to the Duchamp-Villon *Le Cheval* ... makes the value of the piece in the context of our collection strikingly apparent."[1] The Duchamp-Villon had been a gift to the Gallery of Art a year earlier in 1977, also from the Weils, whose collection of cubist art was strong.

The Marlborough-Gerson Gallery in New York, the primary dealer in Lipchitz's work since the death of Curt Valentin in the 1950s, had staged an exhibition of Lipchitz's cubist sculpture from 1913–30 in 1968. The show, featuring sixty-five pieces, included *Pierrot with Clarinet*. Well-established though Lipchitz was by the time of his death in 1973, a retrospective exhibition of his work at the Metropolitan Museum of Art the previous year had further boosted his American reputation. The work's affinity with cubism (it has been compared to Gris' paintings from the mid-1910s) appears to have been its most treasured attribute in 1978. [BF]

1. Gerald D. Bolas to Mrs. Richard K. Weil, November 7, 1978. Washington University Gallery of Art archives.

HENRI MATISSE
(French, 1869–1954)

13
Still Life with Oranges (II), c. 1899
Oil on canvas, 18 ¹/₁₆ x 21 ⁷/₈"
Gift of Mr. and Mrs. Sydney M. Shoenberg, Jr., 1962

Provenance

	Artist
–1951	Boch Collection (The Netherlands)
1951	Theodore Schempp
	(Sale at Hôtel Drouot, Feb. 16, 1951, lot 41)
1951–62	Mr. and Mrs. Sidney M. Shoenberg, Jr.
	(St. Louis, MO)
1962–	Washington University Gallery of Art
	(St. Louis, MO)

When *Still Life with Oranges (II)* was acquired in 1962, no comprehensive exhibition of Henri Matisse's work had been given in the United States since 1951 (Museum of Modern Art), and none would be offered until 1966 (University of California, Los Angeles, Art Galleries). Scholarship on the artist in the late 1950s was dominated by Germany and France, where histories of Matisse by Jacques Lassaigne and Raymond Escholier combined connoisseurship and adulatory biography.[1] These were available in America in 1959 and 1960, when the formalism dominating European accounts was seen as well in contemporary American criticism. The landmark events of 1961 and 1962 were exhibitions of Matisse's late paper cut-outs in Paris and New York, which were reported on in the American press. Reviews of these shows described Matisse's oeuvre along the modernist model of linear development and characterized the artist's genius in terms, akin to those of Clement Greenberg, of "flatness" and disposition of color and pattern.[2] Referring to Matisse as a "rational Romantic" (a term used to characterize his countryman Jean-Paul Sartre), one critic smoothly associated the French artist with the intellectual and transcendental strains of Greenberg's modernism.[3] Descriptions of *Still Life with Oranges (II)* in 1966 reinforced the linear narrative, emphasizing the transitional character of the canvas between "post-impressionist" still life and fauve experimentation.[4] The 1966 reissue of Alfred H. Barr, Jr.'s *Matisse: His Art and his Public* (first published in 1951), concurrent with the Los Angeles exhibition, underscored the view of Matisse's career as a closed history. Barr's narrative, then fifteen years old, was offered to the public without retrospective amendments or elaboration. [GS]

1. Jacques Lassaigne, *Matisse: A Biographical and Critical Study*, trans. Stuart Gilbert (Paris: Editions d'Art Albert Skira, 1959); Raymond Escholier, *Matisse: A Portrait of the Artist and the Man*, trans. Geraldine and H.M. Colvile (New York: Praeger Publishers, 1960).
2. See Pierre Schneider, "Art News from Paris," *Art News* 60, no. 3 (May 1961): p. 44; and Sidney Tillim, "New York Exhibitions: Month in Review," *Arts Magazine* 36, no. 4 (January 1962): pp. 28–30.
3. Tillim, "New York Exhibitions," p. 30.
4. Lawrence Gowing, *Henri Matisse: 64 Paintings* (New York: Museum of Modern Art and Doubleday & Co., 1966), pp. 6–7; and Alfred H. Barr, Jr., *Matisse: His Art and his Public* (New York: Museum of Modern Art and Arno Press, 1966 reprint of 1951 edition), pp. 48–49, 67, 304.

JOAN MIRÓ
(Spanish, 1893–1983)

14

Peinture (Painting), 1925

Oil on linen, 39¹/₂ x 28³/₄"

Gift of Mr. and Mrs. Richard K. Weil, 1963

© 2001 Artists Rights Society (ARS), New York/ADAGP, Paris

Provenance

	Artist
–1959	Hector Brame (Paris, France)
1959–63	Mr. and Mrs. Richard K. Weil (St. Louis, MO)
1963–	Washington University Gallery of Art (St. Louis, MO)

The donation of *Peinture* (1925) to the Washington University Gallery of Art by Mr. and Mrs. Richard K. Weil in 1963 marked the third painting by Joan Miró to enter the collection, following *Peinture of 1933* (cat. no. 15) and *Portrait of J. F. Ràfols* (1917). The Weils had acquired *Peinture* (1925) only four years earlier from Hector Brame of Paris, who appears to have taken possession directly from the artist. Responding to the gift, William Eisendrath, Jr., then curator of the collection, noted that "with this addition, we shall have three most important examples of this most important artist's work–1917, 1925 and 1933."[1] *Peinture* (1925) bridged a sixteen-year gap in the collection's holdings by Miró at its exact midpoint.

In the decade prior to the Weils' donation, Miró's work had been widely exhibited in New York City, including four one-man shows at the Pierre Matisse Gallery and one at the Museum of Modern Art (MOMA) in 1959, the year the Weils purchased *Peinture* (1925) from Matisse. The Washington University painting figured in none of them, but James Thrall Soby, in a monograph on the artist published in conjunction with the MOMA exhibition, called Miró's paintings of the mid-1920s "a superb series of freely organized and relatively abstract works."[2] Soby referred to the gray wash atmospheres of such works as "wavy café-au-lait background[s]." Despite the relatively explicit sexual references in *Peinture* (1925) and some of its related works, figural and linguistic features for Soby amounted simply to "integral element[s] of [Miró's] plastic order." [BF]

1. William Eisendrath, Jr. to Richard K. Weil, July 26, 1963. Washington University Gallery of Art archives.

2. James Thrall Soby, *Joan Miró*, exh. cat. (New York: Museum of Modern Art, 1959), pp. 45–48.

JOAN MIRÓ
(Spanish, 1893–1983)

15
Peinture (Painting), 1933
Oil on canvas mounted on board, 51 15/16 x 77 5/8"
University purchase, Kende Sale Fund, 1945
© 2001 Artists Rights Society (ARS), New York/ADAGP, Paris

Provenance

Artist	
George L. K. Morris (New York, NY)	
Pierre Matisse Gallery (New York, NY)	–1945
Washington University Gallery of Art (St. Louis, MO)	1945–

"Joan Miró is the most important living Spanish painter next to Picasso. . . . However, the St. Louis City Art Museum does not own any examples of his work, and Mr. Nagel, the acting director, believes that [*Peinture* (1933)] would be an important supplement to the Museum's own collection of modern art."[1] Lawrence Hill's recommendation of Miró's *Peinture* (1933) for purchase, based on H. W. Janson's judgment of the piece, seems to speak of the Gallery of Art's simultaneous desires to collaborate and compete with the City Art Museum in building a first-rate collection of modernist art for St. Louis. Both *Peinture* (1933) and Paul Klee's *Überbrückung* (1935; cat. no. 11) entered the collection as a result of Hill's letter of recommendation. The work by Miró appears not to have been publicly exhibited up to that point in its twelve-year history.

Recent scholarship on surrealism has noted that the trend from small, intimate images to larger, sometimes mural-sized canvases broadly corresponds with the artists' shift away from interior, personal subject matter toward more publicly oriented and politically motivated work[2]. In the cases of Pablo Picasso, Salvador Dali, and Miró, this tendency arose primarily through the events leading up to the Spanish civil war. That such a possibility exists in *Peinture* (1933), despite its almost completely nonobjective content, appears to have held no importance for its acquisition in 1945. Hill praised the piece as "one of the artist's largest and most important," but only claimed further that it "display[s] his special qualities of color and line to best advantage."[3] [BF]

1. Lawrence Hill to Arthur H. Compton, November 12, 1945, Washington University Gallery of Art archives.
2. See for example Sam Hunter, John Jacobus, and Daniel Wheeler, *Modern Art: Painting, Sculpture, Architecture* (New York: Prentice Hall, 2000), p. 227, and *Realism, Rationalism, Surrealism: Art Between the Wars*, ed. Briony Fer, David Batchelor, and Paul Wood (New Haven and London: Yale University Press, 1993), pp. 260–62.
3. Hill to Compton, November 12, 1945.

PABLO PICASSO
(Spanish, 1881–1973)

16
Glass and Bottle of Suze, 1912

Pasted papers, gouache and charcoal, 25³/₄ x 19³/₄"

University purchase, Kende Sale Fund, 1946

Provenance

	Artist
	Daniel-Henry Kahnweiler (Paris, France)
	C. Mettler (Paris, France)
–1942	Gallery of Living Art, New York University (New York, NY)
–1946	Bignou Gallery (New York, NY)
1946–	Washington University Gallery of Art (St. Louis, MO)

Before the acquisitions of 1945–46, Washington University's holdings of works by Pablo Picasso amounted to a single drypoint etching of *Salomé* (1905). With the earnings from the Kende sale, Janson and the Art Collection Committee increased that number significantly, adding an aquatint, *Still Life with Lobster* (1945), an etching, *Combat* (1937), and the collage *Glass and Bottle of Suze*. The latter is one of Picasso's best-known collages today, in large part due to political readings of the work by such art historians as Patricia Leighten and Francis Frascina.[1] In the 1940s little distinguished the work from the artist's other two-dimensional paper constructions in the eyes of contemporary viewers. A blurry, half-page photograph of it appears in a 1942 catalogue raisonné of Picasso's works, and it had been exhibited only once by 1941.[2]

As with so many of the works purchased with funds from the Kende sale, *Glass and Bottle of Suze* came to St. Louis via New York. The primary interest of the Art Collection Committee in *La Suze* was its capacity to show the evolution of cubism, which was hailed without question at the time as the most important development in twentieth-century art. Noting that "as a key work in the creation of cubism" the collage "had a special instructive value," critic Reed Hynds praised the acquisition as well-suited to its educational setting.[3] [BF]

1. Patricia Leighten offered one of the earliest readings of the news clippings in *Glass and Bottle of Suze*, placing the collage within a powerful cultural context. See Leighten, "Picasso's Collages and the Threat of War 1912–13," *Art Bulletin* LXVII, no. 4 (December 1985): pp. 653–72. Leighten's political reading of the piece was more widely disseminated by Francis Frascina in his "Realism and Ideology: An Introduction to Semiotics and Cubism," in *Primitivism, Cubism, Abstraction: The Early Twentieth Century*, ed. Charles Harrison, Francis Frascina and Gill Perry (New Haven and London: Yale University Press, 1993), pp. 86–182.

2. *Glass and Bottle of Suze* is no. 422 in Christian Zervos, *Picasso*, 8 vols. (Paris: Cahiers d'Art, 1942), 2, pl. 1197.

3. Reed Hynds, "Yielding Place to New," *Art News* 45, no. 4 (June 1946): p. 63.

PABLO PICASSO
(Spanish, 1881–1973)

17
Les Femmes d'Alger (Women of Algiers),
Variation "N," 1955
Oil on canvas, 45 x 57 5/8"
University purchase, Steinberg Fund, 1960

Provenance	
	Artist
–1956	Galerie Louis Leiris (Paris, France)
1956	Collection Victor and Sally Ganz (New York, NY)
1956–60	Paul Rosenberg and Co. (New York, NY)
1960–	Washington University Gallery of Art (St. Louis, MO)

Only five years old when it arrived in St. Louis, Pablo Picasso's *Les Femmes d'Alger*, variation "N," had already changed hands several times and taken its place among the key works of the artist's later years. This, the penultimate version in a series inspired by Eugène Delacroix's famous painting of the same name from 1834, debuted at Paris' *Musée des Arts Décoratifs* alongside the fourteen other paintings of the series the year Picasso completed them. The exhibition traveled to Munich, Cologne and Hamburg with the entire series still intact, having been acquired by the Galerie Louis Leiris, Paris. The exhibition catalog devoted several pages to these works, identifying the last two, and thus the one that would eventually find a home at Washington University, as the strongest of the group. Both French and German versions of the catalog praised the work for its color and design.[1]

By 1957, when the series (short three for lack of exhibition space) made its public debut in America at the Museum of Modern Art (MOMA), Leiris had sold the suite to Mr. and Mrs. Victor Ganz, who had in turn broken the set among five other American collectors. The MOMA catalog declared that the *Women of Algiers* series, with variation "N" among its strongest parts, "[bore] witness to the sustained invention and vitality of the artist now in his 75th year."[2] When Etta Steinberg purchased variation "N" from Paul Rosenberg to commemorate the 1960 dedication of Washington University's Steinberg Hall (built in part to showcase the University collection in a permanent home on campus), it simultaneously demonstrated the Gallery of Art's commitment to contemporary European trends and its esteem for an established master of twentieth-century modernism. [BF]

1. *Picasso Peintures: 1900–1955*, exh. cat. (Paris: Musée des Arts Décoratifs, 1955), no. 127, and *Picasso: 1900–1955*, exh. cat. (Munich: Franzis-Druck, 1955), no. 121.

2. Alfred H. Barr, Jr., *Picasso: 75th Anniversary Exhibition*, exh. cat. (New York: Museum of Modern Art, 1957), p. 4.

JACKSON POLLOCK
(American, 1912–1956)

18

Sleeping Effort Number 3, 1953
Oil and duco enamel on canvas, 49 ⁷/₈ x 76 ¹/₄"
University purchase, Bixby Fund, 1954

© 2002 The Pollock-Krasner Foundation/Artists Rights Society (ARS), New York

Provenance

Artist	
–1954	Sidney Janis Gallery (New York, NY)
1954–	Washington University Gallery of Art (St. Louis, MO)

When the Washington University Gallery of Art acquired *Sleeping Effort Number 3* in 1954, critics saw in this abstract composition "brutally dissected" human and animal forms and interpreted these as a return to Jackson Pollock's myth paintings of the mid-1940s, such as *Guardians of the Secret* (1943) or *She-Wolf* (1943).[1] The intensity of the image, with its clashing colors and strong, black line, also evoked associations with Pollock's profile at the time as an "angry" and "powerful" artist, a paradigmatic figure of the New York School.[2] At the same time, however, reviewers read this painting and related works of 1953 as being indebted to, among others, Pablo Picasso, Wassily Kandinsky, and Henri Matisse.[3] This common thread in the contemporary response is striking in its effort to align the artist's career with those of the great Europeans while claiming a particularly "American" quality of forceful expression. The ideal of the virile American artist infusing European aesthetics with an energy both physical and creative had existed at least as far back as the 1870s and was enlisted in a general program among artists and critics in the postwar period to claim New York as the capital of art and its native sons as the heroes of a new kind of painting. [GS]

1. Thomas B. Hess, "Jackson Pollock," *Art News* 53, no. 1 (March 1954): p. 40.
2. James Fitzsimmons, "Art Review," *Arts & Architecture* 71, no. 2 (March 1954): p. 7.
3. Ibid., p. 30. See also S. Lane Faison, Jr., "Art," *The Nation* 178, no. 8 (February 20, 1954): pp. 154–56.

YVES TANGUY

(French, 1900–1955)

19

La Tour Marine (Tower of the Sea), 1944

Oil on canvas, 35⁷/₈ x 13³/₄"

University purchase, Kende Sale Fund, 1946

© 2002 Estate of Yves Tanguy/Artists Rights Society (ARS), New York

Provenance

Artist

–1946   Pierre Matisse Gallery (New York, NY)

1946–   Washington University Gallery of Art

(St. Louis, MO)

Yves Tanguy's career in the United States was somewhat more successful than that of his fellow surrealist, Max Ernst. Where Ernst struggled to achieve critical recognition and to find a market for his work, Tanguy was a highly visible figure, with works shown in surrealist exhibitions in commercial galleries and acquired by major American institutions. Unlike Ernst, whose failed marriage to Peggy Guggenheim cut him off from a potentially lucrative venue for his work, Tanguy enjoyed a long-term relationship with the Pierre Matisse Gallery that began in 1939.[1] However, Tanguy shared with Ernst the opprobrium leveled at certain surrealists by Clement Greenberg, America's chief theorist of modern painting. While acknowledging that Tanguy's spectral forms and gloomy atmospherics existed only in the imagination, Greenberg felt the artist's work was too concerned with providing the *illusion* of real objects in space. In this respect, Tanguy, Ernst, and Salvador Dali had led surrealism into a conservative academicism—a fatal flaw that compromised the discipline of "pure painting" and that defined Tanguy's images not as avant-garde, but as "kitsch." Greenberg's preferred model was that of André Masson, Jean Arp, or Joan Miró, the surrealists whose techniques of automatic writing were closer in spirit to the gestural freedom of young Americans such as Jackson Pollock.[2] Although Tanguy publicly asserted that he felt far removed from the war as an exile living in Connecticut,[3] viewers of his paintings felt differently. Writing in 1945, one critic asserted that over Tanguy's recent work lay "the shadow of war" that "goes beyond symbolism into a reality of mental distress. . . ."[4] Another critic shortly thereafter agreed that Tanguy's recent images suggested a world in which life, energy, and playfulness had "turned to vapor."[5] [GS]

1. Sabine Eckmann, "Surrealism in Exile: Responses to the European Destruction of Humanism," in *Exiles and Emigrés: The Flight of European Artists from Hitler*, ed. Stephanie Barron and Sabine Eckmann (Los Angeles and New York: Los Angeles County Museum of Art and Harry N. Abrams, 1997), pp. 170–71.

2. Clement Greenberg, "Surrealist Painting," *The Nation* 159, nos. 7, 8 (August 12 and 19, 1944): pp. 192–93, 219–20.

3. Yves Tanguy, as quoted in an interview with James Johnson Sweeney, "Eleven Europeans in America," *Museum of Modern Art Bulletin* 13, nos. 4, 5 (1946): p. 22.

4. Margaret Breuning, "Surrealist Disillusion of Yves Tanguy," *Art Digest* 19, no. 16 (May 15, 1945): p. 9.

5. "Reviews and Previews," *Art News* 45, no. 9 (November 1946): p. 44.

THEO VAN DOESBURG

(Dutch, 1883–1931)

20

Composition VII: The Three Graces, 1917

Oil on canvas, 33 $\frac{1}{2}$ x 33 $\frac{1}{2}$"

University purchase, Yeatman Fund, 1947

Provenance

–c. 1921   Artist
                       Lena Milius

–1947   Collection Mme. van Doesburg
                       (Maidon, France)

1947–   Washington University Gallery of Art
                       (St. Louis, MO) via Art of This Century Gallery
                       (New York, NY)

When *Composition VII: The Three Graces* was purchased in 1947, Theo van Doesburg's cool, highly rationalized, and theoretical art was not "of the moment" in postwar painting, when mythic content and heroic brushwork dominated. Nevertheless, the inclusion of the work in a retrospective 1946 show at the influential Art of This Century Gallery in New York testified to the artist's importance as a founding member of the utopian De Stijl group. De Stijl's standing in the United States had benefitted in recent years from the visibility of van Doesburg's colleague, Piet Mondrian, whose canvases fused the energies of the American urban scene with restrained, geometric abstraction. With Mondrian's death in 1945, the impact of De Stijl was perhaps seen as a closed chapter of modern art history. Certainly, the rarity of fine De Stijl works was recognized by the University's Art Collection Committee.[1] The purchase of *Composition VII: The Three Graces* directly from the retrospective exhibition was in tune with the University's acknowledged program of creating an educational collection of examples of the most significant modern art movements.[2] [GS]

1. Lawrence Hill to Arthur H. Compton, April 15, 1947. Washington University Gallery of Art archives.

2. Reed Hynds, "Yielding Place to New," *Art News* 45, no. 4 (June 1946): pp. 62–63.

MAX BECKMANN
Les Artistes mit Gemüse, 1943

Major Exhibitions

1945 Title unknown, Amsterdam

1946 *Beckmann: His Recent Work from 1939 to 1945*, Buchholz Gallery (New York, NY)

1946 *Works of Max Beckmann*, School of the Museum of Fine Arts (Boston, MA); San Francisco Museum of Modern Art (San Francisco, CA)

1947 One-man show, Philadelphia Art Alliance (Philadelphia, PA)

1948 *Max Beckmann, 1948: Retrospective Exhibition*, City Art Museum (St. Louis, MO); Los Angeles County Museum of Art (Los Angeles, CA); Detroit Institute of Arts (Detroit, MI); Baltimore Museum of Art (Baltimore, MD); Germanic Museum, Harvard University (Cambridge, MA); Minneapolis Institute of Arts (Minneapolis, MN)

1951 *Memorial Exhibition*, venue unknown (Munich, Germany)

1966 *From Daumier to Pollock*, William Rockhill Nelson Gallery of Art - Mary Atkins Museum of Fine Arts (Kansas City, MO)

1968 *From El Greco to Pollock*, Baltimore Museum of Art (Baltimore, MD)

1981 *Westkunst*, Museum Ludwig (Cologne, Germany)

1984 *Max Beckmann Retrospective*, Haus der Kunst (Munich, Germany); Nationalgalerie (Berlin, Germany); The Saint Louis Art Museum (St. Louis, MO); Los Angeles County Museum of Art (Los Angeles, CA)

1994 *Max Beckmann: Masterpieces from St. Louis*, Staatsgalerie (Stuttgart, Germany)

1997 *Exiles and Emigrés: The Flight of European Artists from Hitler*, Los Angeles County Museum of Art (Los Angeles, CA); Montreal Museum of Fine Arts (Montreal, Canada); Neue Nationalgalerie Berlin (Berlin, Germany)

Select Bibliography

Barron, Stephanie, and Sabine Eckmann, eds. *Exiles and Emigrés: The Flight of European Artists from Hitler*. Exhibition catalog. Los Angeles and New York: Los Angeles County Museum of Art and Harry N. Abrams, 1997, pp. 61–62, fig. 38.

Beckett, Wendy. *Beckmann and the Self*. New York: Prestel, 1997, pp. 66–68.

Beckmann: His Recent Work from 1939–1945. Exhibition catalog. New York: Buchholz Gallery, 1946, no. 2.

Defty, Sally Bixby. *The First Hundred Years 1879–1979*. Exhibition catalog. St. Louis: Washington University School of Art, 1979.

Eisendrath, William, N., Jr. "The Washington University Collections." *College Art Journal* 23, no. 4 (Summer 1964): p. 294.

Erpel, Fritz. *Max Beckmann: Leben im Werk, Die Selbstbildnisse*. Berlin: Henschelverlag Kunst und Gesellschaft, 1985, no. 177, pl. 190.

Göpel, Erhard, and Barbara Göpel, eds. *Max Beckmann: Katalog der Gemälde*. 2 volumes. Bern: Kornfeld & Cie., 1976.

Haftmann, Werner. *Painting in the 20th Century*. New York: Frederick A. Praeger, 1960, pl. 687.

———. *Verfemte Kunst*. Köln: Dumont Buchverlag, 1986, p. 60.

Haxthausen, Charles W. "Max Beckmann, *Les Artistes mit Gemüse* (*Artists with Vegetable*) or *Four Men Around a Table*." In Ketner, Joseph, ed. *A Gallery of Modern Art at Washington University in St. Louis*. St. Louis: Washington University Gallery of Art, 1994, pp. 102–3.

Hynds, Reed. "Yielding Place to New." *Art News* 45, no. 4 (June 1946), p. 62.

Janson, H. W. "Modern Art in the Washington University Collection." *Bulletin of the City Art Museum of St. Louis* 32 (March 1947), no. 2.

Lackner, Stephan. *Beckmann*. New York: Harry N. Abrams, 1991, p. 35.

Max Beckmann. Exhibition catalog. St. Louis: City Art Museum, 1948, p. 70.

Myers, Bernard S. *The German Expressionists–A Generation in Revolt*. New York: Frederick A. Praeger, 1957, pl. 61.

Rathbone, Perry T. "*Les Artistes mit Gemüse* (Vier Männer um einen Tisch)." In *Max Beckmann Meisterwerke*. Exhibition catalog. Stuttgart: Staatsgalerie, 1994, pp. 144–45.

Schulz-Hoffman, Carla and Judith C. Weiss, eds. *Max Beckmann Retrospective*. Exhibition catalog. Munich: Haus der Kunst and Prestel-Verlag, 1984, pp. 286–88.

Selz, Peter. *Max Beckmann: The Self-Portraits*. New York: Rizzoli, 1992, p. 82.

———. *Modern Masters: Max Beckmann*. New York: Abbeville Press, 1996, pp. 73–75.

GEORGES BRAQUE
Nature Morte et Verre, 1930

Major Exhibitions

1930   Title unknown, Paul Rosenberg and Co. (Paris, France)

1933   *Georges Braque,* Kunsthalle Basel (Switzerland)

1936   Title unknown, National Museums (Oslo, Norway; Stockholm, Sweden; Helsinki, Finland; Copenhagen, Denmark)

1937   Title unknown, National Museum (Belgrade, Yugoslavia)

1937   Title unknown, Municipal Museum (Amsterdam, The Netherlands)

1937   Title unknown, Palais des Beaux Arts (Brussels, Belgium)

1938   Title unknown, Rosenberg & Helft (London, England)

1938   Title unknown, Kunsthaus (Zurich, Switzerland)

1940   Title unknown, Paul Rosenberg and Company (Paris, France)

1947   *Seeing the Unseeable,* Addison Gallery of American Art, Phillips Academy (Andover, MA)

1964   *Braque (1882–1963): An American Tribute, The Thirties,* Paul Rosenberg and Co. (New York, NY)

1966   *From Daumier to Pollock,* William Rockhill Nelson Gallery of Art - Mary Atkins Museum of Fine Arts (Kansas City, MO)

1988   *Georges Braque,* Isetan Museum of Art, Shinjuku (Tokyo, Japan); Fukuoka Art Museum (Fukuoka, Japan); Shizuoka Prefectural Museum of Art (Shizuoka, Japan); Sogo Museum of Art (Yokohama, Japan)

1990   *Braque: Still Lifes and Interiors,* Walker Art Gallery (Liverpool, England); Bristol Museum and Art Gallery (Bristol, England)

Select Bibliography

Braque: Still Lifes and Interiors. Exhibition catalog. London: South Bank Center, 1990, p. 44.

Catalogue de l'Oeuvre de Georges Braque: 1928–1935. Paris: Maeght, 1962, p. 49.

Einstein, Carl. *Georges Braque.* Paris: Editions des Chroniques du Jour, 1934, pl. 83.

"Georges Braque." *Cahiers d'Art* 8, nos. 1–2 (1933), p. 64.

Golding, John. "Georges Braque, *Still Life with Glass.*" In Ketner, Joseph D., et al. *A Gallery of Modern Art at Washington University in St. Louis.* St. Louis: Washington University Gallery of Art, 1994, pp. 80–81.

Hayes, Bartlett, Jr. *Seeing the Unseeable.* Exhibition catalog. Andover, MA: Addison Gallery of American Art, 1947.

Illustrated Checklist of the Collection: Paintings, Sculpture and Works on Paper. St. Louis: Washington University Gallery of Art, 1981, p. 21.

Janson, H. W. "Modern Art in the Washington University Collection." *Bulletin of the City Art Museum of St. Louis* 32, no. 1 (March 1947), p. 21.

–––. "The New Art Collection at Washington University." *College Art Journal* 6, no. 3 (Spring 1947), p. 204.

Richardson, John, ed. *Georges Braque (1882–1963): An American Tribute.* New York: Public Education Association, 1964, fig. 3.

Weisberg, Gabriel P. *Georges Braque (1882–1963).* Exhibition catalog. Isetan Museum of Art, Japan. Tokyo: Art Life, Ltd., 1988, pl. 19.

Whitmer, T. Carl. "A Composer Looks at Painting." *Creative Art* 10, no. 2 (February 1932), p. 121.

ALEXANDER CALDER
Bayonets Menacing a Flower, 1945

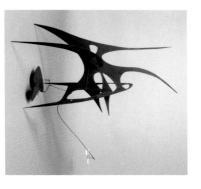

Major Exhibitions

1945   *Alexander Calder*, Buchholz Gallery (New York, NY)

1962   *Alexander Calder*, Tate Gallery (London, England)

1965   *Alexander Calder Retrospective*, Solomon R. Guggenheim Museum (New York, NY); Washington University Gallery of Art (St. Louis, MO)

1966   *From Daumier to Pollock*, William Rockhill Nelson Gallery of Art - Mary Atkins Museum of Fine Art (Kansas City, MO)

1986   *Alexander Calder: An American Invention*, Sheldon Memorial Art Gallery (Lincoln, NE)

1998   *Alexander Calder, 1898-1976*, National Gallery of Art (Washington, DC); San Francisco Museum of Modern Art (San Francisco, CA)

Select Bibliography

Alexander Calder: An American Invention. Exhibition catalog. Lincoln, NE: Sheldon Memorial Art Gallery, 1986.

Hynds, Reed. "Yielding Place to New." *Art News* 45, no. 4 (June 1946), p. 62.

Janson, H. W. "Modern Art in the Washington University Collection." *Bulletin of the City Art Museum of St. Louis* 32, no. 1 (March 1947), no. 25.

Marter, Joan M., "Alexander Calder, *Bayonets Menacing a Flower*." In Ketner, Joseph D., et al. *A Gallery of Modern Art at Washington University in St. Louis.* St. Louis: Washington University Gallery of Art, 1994, pp. 162–63.

–––. *Alexander Calder.* Cambridge, MA: Cambridge University Press, 1991, p. 214.

Prather, Marla. *Alexander Calder, 1898–1976.* Washington D.C.: National Gallery of Art, 1998, p. 225, fig. 190.

Sweeney, James Johnson. *Alexander Calder.* New York: Museum of Modern Art, 1951, pp. 61–62.

–––. *Alexander Calder.* Exhibition catalog, Tate Gallery, London: The Arts Council of Great Britain, 1962, p. 43, no. 38.

WILLEM DE KOONING
Saturday Night, 1956

Major Exhibitions

1956   *Willem de Kooning*, Sidney Janis Gallery (New York, NY)

1962   *Art Since 1950, American and International*, Fine Arts Pavilion, World's Fair (Seattle, WA); Rose Art Museum, Brandeis University (Waltham, MA)

1964   *American Painting 1910-1960*, Indiana University (Bloomington, IN)

1969   *Willem de Kooning*, Museum of Modern Art (New York, NY); Art Institute of Chicago (Chicago, IL); Los Angeles County Museum of Art (Los Angeles, CA)

1974   *Poets of the Cities, New York and San Francisco 1950–65*, Dallas Museum of Fine Arts (Dallas, TX); Pollock Galleries, Southern Methodist University (Dallas, TX); San Francisco Museum of Art, (San Francisco, CA); Wadsworth Atheneum (Hartford, CT)

1987   *Abstract Expressionism: The Critical Developments*, Albright-Knox Art Gallery (Buffalo, NY)

1994   *Willem de Kooning: Paintings*, National Gallery of Art (Washington D.C.); Metropolitan Museum of Art (New York, NY); Tate Gallery (London, England)

Select Bibliography

Art Since 1950, American and International. Exhibition catalog. Seattle: Seattle World's Fair, 1962, p. 18.

Auping, Michael. *Abstract Expressionism: The Critical Developments.* Exhibition catalog. Buffalo and New York: Albright-Knox Art Gallery and Harry N. Abrams, 1987, p. 200, fig. 36.

Gaugh, Harry F. *Willem de Kooning.* New York: Abbeville Press, 1983, pp. 56, 131, fig. 113.

Hess, Thomas B. "Selecting from the Flow of Spring Shows: Willem de Kooning." *Art News* 55, no. 2 (April 1956), pp. 24–25, 100.

———. *Willem de Kooning.* New York: G. Braziller, 1959, p. 152.

———. *Willem de Kooning.* Exhibition catalog. New York: Museum of Modern Art, 1969, p. 106.

Janis, Harriet and Rudi Blesh. *De Kooning.* New York: Grove Press, 1960, p. 142.

Poets of the Cities: New York and San Francisco, 1950–1965. Exhibition catalog. Dallas and New York: Dallas Museum of Fine Arts and E. P. Dutton & Company, 1974, pl. 3.

Prather, Marla, et al. *Willem de Kooning: Painting.* New Haven: Yale University Press, 1994, pl. 151.

Rand, Harry. "Willem de Kooning, *Saturday Night.*" In Ketner, Joseph D., et al. *A Gallery of Modern Art at Washington University in St. Louis.* St. Louis: Washington University Gallery of Art, 1994, pp. 176–77.

Rosenberg, Harold. *De Kooning.* New York: Harry N. Abrams, 1974, p. 33. pl. 117.

Solomon, Alan. *Painting in New York: 1944-1969.* Exhibition catalog. Pasadena: Pasadena Art Museum, 1969, pp. 37, 70.

Yard, Sally. *Willem de Kooning.* New York: Rizzoli, 1997, p. 63.

JEAN DUBUFFET

Poches aux Yeux, 1959

Major Exhibitions

1962   *Dubuffet, Museum of Modern Art* (New York, NY)

1984   *Jean Dubuffet: Forty Years of his Art,* The David
        and Alfred Smart Gallery, The University of Chicago
        (Chicago, IL); The Washington University Gallery
        of Art (St. Louis, MO)

Select Bibliography

Franzke, Andreas. *Jean Dubuffet: Petites Statues de la Vie
Précaire.* Bern: Verlag Gachnang and Springer, 1988, pp. 33,
226, no. 57.

Loreau, Max. *Catalogue des Travaux de Jean Dubuffet:
Fascicule XVII, Materiologies.* Lausanne, Switzerland: Weber,
1969, pp. 10, 70, no. 78.

———. *Jean Dubuffet: Délits, Déportements, Lieux de Haut
Jeu.* Lausanne, Switzerland: Imprimeries Réunies, 1971, p. 335.

Messer, Thomas M. "Jean Dubuffet, *Poches aux Yeux.*" In
Ketner, Joseph D., et al. *A Gallery of Modern Art at
Washington University in St. Louis.* St. Louis: Washington
University Gallery of Art, 1994, pp. 128–29.

Major Exhibitions

1960 *Dubuffet*, World House Gallery (New York, NY)

1962 *Dubuffet*, Museum of Modern Art (New York, NY)

1984 *Jean Dubuffet: Forty Years of his Art*, The David and Alfred Smart Gallery, The University of Chicago (Chicago, IL); The Washington University Gallery of Art (St. Louis, MO)

1993 *Jean Dubuffet, 1943–1963: Paintings, Sculptures, Assemblages*, Hirschhorn Museum and Sculpture Garden, Smithsonian Institution (Washington, DC)

Select Bibliography

Franzke, Andreas. *Jean Dubuffet: Petites Statues de la Vie Précaire*. Bern: Verlag Gachnang and Springer, 1988, pp. 31, 227, no. 62.

Jean Dubuffet. Exhibition catalog. New York: World House Gallery, 1960, no. 40.

Jean Dubuffet, 1943–1963: Paintings, Sculptures, Assemblages. Exhibition catalog. Washington, DC: Hirshhorn Museum and Sculpture Garden/Smithsonian Institute Press, 1993, p. 128, no. 82.

Loreau, Max. *Catalogue des Travaux de Jean Dubuffet: Fascicule XVII, Materiologies*. Lausanne, Switzerland: Weber, 1969, p. 73, no. 83.

–––. *Jean Dubuffet: Délits, Déportements, Lieux de Haut Jeu*. Lausanne, Switzerland: Imprimeries Réunies, 1971, p. 336.

Messer, Thomas M. "Jean Dubuffet, *Tête Barbue*." In Ketner, Joseph D., et al. *A Gallery of Modern Art at Washington University in St. Louis*. St. Louis: Washington University Gallery of Art, 1994, pp. 130–31.

Pieyre de Mandiargues, André. "Des Barbes et des Feuilles." *XXe Siecle* 22 (June 1960), p. 9.

Selz, Peter. *The Work of Jean Dubuffet*. Exhibition catalog. New York: Museum of Modern Art, 1962, p. 154.

JEAN DUBUFFET
Tête Barbue, 1959

MAX ERNST

The Eye of Silence, 1943–44

Major Exhibitions

1944   *Painting in the U.S.*, Carnegie Institute (Pittsburgh, PA)

1945   *European Artists in America*, Whitney Museum of American Art (New York, NY)

1946   *17th Exhibition of Contemporary American Oil Painting*, Cleveland Museum of Art (Cleveland, OH)

1954   *Venice Biennale* (Venice, Italy)

1961   *Max Ernst*, Museum of Modern Art (New York, NY); Art Institute of Chicago (Chicago, IL)

1964   *Constant Companions Show*, University of St. Thomas (Houston, TX)

1966   *From Daumier to Pollock*, William Rockhill Nelson Gallery of Art - Mary Atkins Museum of Fine Arts (Kansas City, MO)

1971   Title unknown, Orangerie des Tuileries (Paris, France)

1973   *20th Century Masterworks from St. Louis Collections*, The Saint Louis Art Museum (St. Louis, MO)

1975   *Max Ernst Retrospective*, Guggenheim Museum (New York, NY); Grand Palais (Paris, France)

1991   *Max Ernst*, Tate Gallery (London, England); Staatsgalerie (Stuttgart, Germany); Kunstsammlung Nordrhein-Westfalen (Dusseldorf, Germany); Musée National d'Art Moderne (Paris, France); Centre Georges Pompidou (Paris, France)

1997   *Exiles and Emigrés*, Los Angeles County Museum of Art (Los Angeles, CA); Montreal Museum of Fine Art (Montreal, Canada); Neue Nationalgalerie Berlin (Berlin, Germany)

1997   *The Dual Muse: The Writer As Artist, The Artist As Writer*, Washington University Gallery of Art (St. Louis, MO)

1999   *Max Ernst: Die Retrospektive*, Neue Nationalgalerie (Berlin, Germany); Haus der Kunst (Munich, Germany)

Select Bibliography

Barron, Stephanie, and Sabine Eckmann, eds. *Exiles and Emigrés: The Flight of European Artists from Hitler*. Exhibition catalog. Los Angeles and New York: Los Angeles County Museum of Art and Harry N. Abrams, 1997, pl. 37.

La Biennale di Venezia, Le Esposizioni Internazionali d'Arte, 1895–1995: Artisti, Mostre, Partecipazioni Nazionali, Premi. Venice and Milan: La Biennale di Venezia and Electa, 1996, p. 254.

Bischoff, Ulrich. *Max Ernst, 1891–1976, Jenseits der Malerei*. Köln: Benedikt Taschen Verlag GmbH, 1987, p. 74.

Breton, André. *Le Peinture et le Surréalisme*. New York: Brentanos, 1945, p. 56.

European Artists in America. Exhibition catalog. New York: Whitney Museum of American Art, 1945.

Homburg, Cornelia, ed. *The Dual Muse: The Writer As Artist, The Artist As Writer*. Exhibition catalog. St. Louis and Amsterdam: Washington University Gallery of Art and John Benjamins Publishing, 1997, p. 17.

Hynds, Reed. "Yielding Place to New." *Art News* 45, no. 4 (June 1946), p. 63.

Janson, H. W. "Modern Art in the Washington University Collection." *Bulletin of the City Art Museum of St. Louis* 32, no. 1 (March 1947), p. 25.

Lieberman, William S., ed. *Max Ernst*. Exhibition catalog. New York: Museum of Modern Art, 1961, p. 42–43.

Maurer, Evan M. "Max Ernst, *The Eye of Silence*." In Ketner, Joseph D., et al. *A Gallery of Modern Art at Washington University in St. Louis*. St. Louis: Washington University Gallery of Art, 1994, pp. 118–19.

Max Ernst. Exhibition catalog. Paris: Orangerie des Tuileries, 1971, p. 25, pl. 18.

"Notable Works of Art Now on the Market." *Art News* 44, no. 4 (April 1, 1945), p. 41.

Painting in the USA. Exhibition catalog. Pittsburgh: Carnegie Institute, 1944, p. 98.

Riley, Maude. "Ernst's Latest Work." *Art Digest* 19, no. 16 (May 1945), p. 7.

Schneede, Uwe M. *Max Ernst*. Stuttgart: Verlag Gerd Hatje GmbH, 1972, p. 174.

Spies, Werner. *Max Ernst*. Exhibition catalog. Paris: Centre Georges Pompidou, 1991, p. 256.

———. *Max Ernst: Die Retrospektive*. Exhibition catalog. Munich: Haus der Kunst and Dumont, 1999, pp. 128, 184.

Veseley, Dalibor. "Surrealism, Myth, and Modernity." *Architectural Design* 48, nos. 2–3 (1978), p. 90.

ARSHILE GORKY
Golden Brown, 1943–44

Major Exhibitions

1951   Title unknown, Whitney Museum of American Art (New York, NY); Walker Art Center (Minneapolis, MN); San Francisco Museum (San Francisco, CA)

1953   *Arshile Gorky in the Final Years*, Sidney Janis Gallery (New York, NY)

1962   *Arshile Gorky Retrospective*, Museum of Modern Art (New York, NY)

1994   *Arshile Gorky: A Ninetieth Birthday Commemoration*, Gagosian Gallery (New York, NY)

1995   *Arshile Gorky: The Breakthrough Years*, National Gallery of Art (Washington, DC); Albright-Knox Art Gallery (Buffalo, NY); Modern Art Museum of Fort Worth (St. Worth, TX)

Select Bibliography

Auping, Michael. *Arshile Gorky: The Breakthrough Years.* Exhibition catalog. Ft. Worth and New York: Modern Art Museum of Fort Worth and Rizzoli, 1995, pp. 112–13, pl. 12.

De Kooning, Elaine. "Gorky: Painter of his Own Legend." *Art News* 49, no. 1 (January 1951), p. 66.

Dennison, George. "The Crisis Art of Arshile Gorky." *Arts* 37 (February 1963), p. 18.

Jordan, Jim M., and Robert Goldwater. *The Paintings of Arshile Gorky: A Critical Catalogue.* New York and London: New York University Press, 1982, pp. 416–17.

Lader, Melvin. *Arshile Gorky.* New York: Abbeville Press, 1985, p. 77, pl. 71.

Rand, Harry. *Arshile Gorky: The Implication of Symbols.* Montclair, NJ: Allanheld, Osman, and Company, 1981, p. 126, pls. 8–15.

———. "Gorky in Virginia." *Arts in Virginia* 26, no. 1 (1986), p. 12, pl. 14.

———. "Arshile Gorky, *Golden Brown*." In Ketner, Joseph D., et al. *A Gallery of Modern Art at Washington University in St. Louis.* St. Louis: Washington University Gallery of Art, 1994, pp. 172–73.

Seitz, William Chapin. *Arshile Gorky: Paintings, Drawings, Studies.* Exhibition catalog. New York: Museum of Modern Art, 1962, pp. 54–55.

Spender, Matthew. *From a High Place: The Life of Arshile Gorky.* New York: Alfred A. Knopf, 1999, pp. 243–44, pl. 245.

JUAN GRIS

Still Life with Playing Cards, 1916

Major Exhibitions

1929   *School of Paris, 1910–1928*, Harvard Society for Contemporary Art (Cambridge, MA)

1944   *Juan Gris Retrospective*, Buchholz Gallery (New York, NY) (listed as *Checker Board and Glass*)

1946   *Four Spaniards*, Boston Museum of Fine Arts (Boston, MA)

1947   *French Painting*, Indiana University Art Museum (Bloomington, IN)

1948   *Juan Gris*, Cincinnati Modern Art Society (Cincinnati, OH)

1948   *Spanish Masters of the 20th Century*, San Francisco Museum of Art (San Francisco, CA); Portland Museum of Art (Portland, ME)

1958   *Juan Gris*, Museum of Modern Art (New York, NY); Minnesota Institute of the Arts (Minneapolis, MN); San Francisco Museum of Art (San Francisco, CA); Los Angeles County Museum (Los Angeles, CA)

1966   *Fifty Years of Modern Art*, Cleveland Museum of Art (Cleveland, OH)

1974   *Celebration*, Museum of Art, Carnegie Institute (Pittsburgh, PA)

Select Bibliography

Cooper, Douglas. *Juan Gris*. Paris: Berggruen, 1977, pp. 282–83.

Hynds, Reed. "Yielding Place to New." *Art News* 45, no. 4 (June 1946), pp. 32, 63.

Ittmann, William. *Juan Gris 1887–1927*. Exhibition catalog. St. Louis: Washington University Gallery of Art, 1966, p. 1.

Janson, H. W. "The New Art Collection at Washington University." *College Art Journal* 6, no. 3 (Spring 1947), p. 200.

——. "Modern Art in the Washington University Collection." *Bulletin of the City Art Museum of St. Louis* 32, no. 1 (March 1947), no. 9.

Juan Gris Retrospective. Exhibition catalog. New York: Buchholz Gallery, 1944, no. 8.

Kahnweiler, Daniel-Henry. *Juan Gris: His Life and Work*. London: Lund-Humphries, 1947, pl. 30.

Modern Masters of Spanish Painting: Legacy of Spain, 20th Century. Exhibition catalog. San Diego: Fine Arts Gallery, 1969.

Rosenthal, Mark. "Juan Gris, *Still Life with Playing Cards* (*Draughts Board and Playing Cards*)." In Ketner, Joseph D., et al. *A Gallery of Modern Art at Washington University in St. Louis*. St. Louis: Washington University Gallery of Art, 1994, pp. 84–85.

Soby, James Thrall. *Juan Gris*. Exhibition catalog. New York: Museum of Modern Art, 1958, pp. 61, 67.

Years of Ferment. Exhibition catalog. Los Angeles: University of California at Los Angeles Art Council, 1965, p. 54, no 58.

Zervos, Christian. *Histoire de l'Art Contemporaine*. Paris: Editions Cahiers d'Art, 1938, p. 291.

MARSDEN HARTLEY
The Iron Cross, 1915

Major Exhibitions

1915 One-man show, Haas-Heye Galerie Münchner Graphik-Verlag (Berlin, Germany)

1916 *Hartley Exposition,* Photosecession Gallery "291" (New York, NY)

1951 *Revolution and Tradition in American Art,* Brooklyn Museum of Art (New York, NY)

1962 *Stieglitz & his Circle,* Museum of Modern Art (New York, NY)

1968 *Marsden Hartley, Painter/Poet,* University of Southern California (Los Angeles, CA); Tucson Art Center (Tucson, AZ); University of Texas at Austin (Austin, TX)

1980 *Marsden Hartley,* Whitney Museum of American Art (New York, NY); Art Institute of Chicago (Chicago, IL); The Saint Louis Art Museum (St. Louis, MO); Amon Carter Museum (Fort Worth, TX); University Art Museum, University of California at Berkeley (Berkeley, CA)

1984 *In Quest of Excellence: Civic Pride, Patronage, Connoisseurship,* Center for Fine Arts (Miami, FL)

1995 *Dictated By Life: Marsden Hartley and Robert Indiana,* Frederick R. Weisman Art Museum, University of Minnesota (Minneapolis, MN); Terra Museum of American Art (Chicago. IL)

1998 *Marsden Hartley: Modern American Visionary,* Ackland Art Museum, The University of North Carolina at Chapel Hill (Chapel Hill, NC)

2001 *Modern Art and America: Alfred Stieglitz and his New York Galleries,* National Gallery of Art (Washington, D.C.)

Select Bibliography

Bohan, Ruth L. "Marsden Hartley, *The Iron Cross.*" In Ketner, Joseph D., et al. *A Gallery of Modern Art at Washington University in St. Louis.* St. Louis: Washington University Gallery of Art, 1994, pp. 152–53.

Greenough, Sarah. *Modern Art and America: Alfred Stieglitz and his New York Galleries.* Exhibition catalog. Washington, DC and Boston: National Gallery of Art and Bulfinch Press, 2000, p. 239, fig. 74.

Haskell, Barbara. *Marsden Hartley.* Exhibition catalog. New York: Whitney Museum of American Art and New York University Press, 1980, pl. 83.

Levin, Gail. "Hidden Symbolism in Marsden Hartley's Military Pictures." *Arts* 54, no. 2 (October 1979), p. 157.

Ludington, Townsend. *Seeking the Spiritual: The Paintings of Marsden Hartley.* Ithaca: Cornell University Press, 1998, p. 33.

McDonnell, Patricia. *Dictated By Life: Marsden Hartley and Robert Indiana.* Exhibition catalog. Minneapolis and New York: Frederick R. Weisman Art Museum and Distributed Art Publishers, 1995, p. 50.

Plagens, Peter. "Marsden Hartley Revisited." *Artforum* 7, no. 9 (May 1969), pp. 42–43.

Selz, Peter Howard, ed. *Seven Decades, 1895–1965: Crosscurrents in Modern Art.* New York: Public Education Association of the City of New York, 1966, fig. 123.

Van der Marck, Jan. *In Quest of Excellence: Civic Pride, Patronage, Connoisseurship.* Exhibition catalog. Miami: The Trustees of the Center for the Fine Arts Association, 1983, pp. 192, 199.

PAUL KLEE
Überbrückung, 1935

Major Exhibitions

1966   *Paul Klee 1879–1940*, Solomon R. Guggenheim Museum (New York, NY); Pasadena Art Museum (Pasadena, CA); San Francisco Museum of Art (San Francisco, CA); Gallery of Fine Arts (Columbus, OH); Cleveland Museum of Art (Cleveland, OH); William Rockhill Nelson Gallery of Art - Mary Atkins Museum of Fine Arts (Kansas City, MO); Baltimore Museum of Art (Baltimore, MD); Washington University Gallery of Art (St. Louis, MO); Philadelphia Museum of Art (Philadelphia, PA)

1973   *20th Century Masterworks from St. Louis Collections*, The Saint Louis Art Museum (St. Louis, MO)

Select Bibliography

Hynds, Reed. "Yielding Place to New." *Art News* 45, no. 4 (June 1946), p. 62.

Janson, H. W. "Modern Art in the Washington University Collection." *Bulletin of the City Art Museum of St. Louis* 32, no. 1 (March 1947), no. 12.

Kagan, Andrew. "Paul Klee, *Überbrückung (Transition)*." In Ketner, Joseph D., et al. *A Gallery of Modern Art at Washington University in St. Louis*. St. Louis: Washington University Gallery of Art, 1994, pp. 100–101.

Paul Klee 1879–1940: A Retrospective Exhibition. Exhibition catalog. New York and Pasadena: Solomon R. Guggenheim Museum and the Pasadena Art Museum, 1967, p. 101, no. 147.

JACQUES LIPCHITZ
Pierrot with Clarinet, 1919

Major Exhibitions

1968   *Lipchitz: The Cubist Period, 1913–1930*,
Marlborough-Gerson Gallery (New York, NY)

1990   *The Mask of Comedy, The Art of the Italian
Comedia*, J. B. Speed Art Museum (Louisville, KY)

Select Bibliography

Stott, Deborah A. *Jacques Lipchitz and Cubism.* Dissertation.
New York: Columbia University, 1975, pp. 153–54, fig. 41.

Wilkinson, Alan G. "Jacques Lipchitz, *Pierrot with Clarinet*." In
Ketner, Joseph D., et al. *A Gallery of Modern Art at Washington University in St. Louis.* St. Louis: Washington University
Gallery of Art, 1994, pp. 90–91

––––. *The Sculpture of Jacques Lipchitz, a Catalogue: Volume
I, The Paris Years, 1910–1940.* London: Thames and Hudson,
1996, pp. 51, 216.

HENRI MATISSE

Still Life with Oranges (II), c. 1899

Major Exhibitions

1968   *Matisse 1869–1954: A Retrospective Exhibition,* Tate Gallery (London, England)

1992   *Henri Matisse: A Retrospective,* Museum of Modern Art (New York, NY)

1995   *Matisse,* Queensland Art Gallery (Queensland, Australia); National Gallery of Australia (Canberra, Australia); National Gallery of Victoria (Melbourne, Australia)

Select Bibliography

Barr, Alfred H., Jr. *Matisse: His Art and his Public.* New York: Museum of Modern Art and Arno Press, 1951, reprint 1966, pp. 48, 67.

Elderfield, John. *Henri Matisse: A Retrospective.* New York: Museum of Modern Art, 1992, p. 103.

Flam, Jack, ed. *Matisse.* New York: Hugh Lauter Levin Associates, 1988, p. 35.

———. "Henri Matisse, *Still Life with Oranges (II)*." In Ketner, Joseph D., et al. *A Gallery of Modern Art at Washington University in St. Louis.* St. Louis: Washington University Gallery of Art, 1994, pp. 74–75.

Matisse: Ajaccio-Toulouse 1898-1899, Une Saison de Peinture. Toulouse: Musée d'Art Moderne de Toulouse, 1986, p. 80.

Milner, Frank. *Henri Matisse.* London: Bison Books, 1994, pp. 34–35.

Turner, Caroline, and Roger Benjamin. *Matisse.* Exhibition catalog. Queensland and New South Wales: Queensland Art Gallery and Art Exhibitions Australia Limited, 1995, pp. 169, 171, fig. 5.

Watkins, Nicholas. *Matisse.* New York: Oxford University Press, 1985, pp. 37–38.

Wilson, Sarah. *Matisse.* New York: Rizzoli, 1992, p. 9, fig. 12.

109

Major Exhibitions

1965 *Miró in St. Louis*, City Art Museum (St. Louis, MO)

1973 *20th Century Masterworks from St. Louis Collections*, The Saint Louis Art Museum (St. Louis, MO)

1980 *Joan Miró: The Development of a Sign Language*, Washington University Gallery of Art (St. Louis, MO); The David and Alfred Smart Gallery, University of Chicago (Chicago, IL)

1980 *Miró: Selected Paintings*, Albright-Knox Art Gallery (Buffalo, NY)

Select Bibliography

Dupin, Jacques, and Ariane Lelong-Mainaud. *Joan Miró, Catalogue Raisonné. Painting, Volume I: 1908–1930*. Paris: Daniel Lelong, 1999, p. 132, no. 158.

Lubar, Robert S. "Joan Miró, *Joie*." In Ketner, Joseph D., et al. *A Gallery of Modern Art at Washington University in St. Louis*. St. Louis: Washington University Gallery of Art, 1994, pp. 114–15.

Stich, Sidra. *Joan Miró: The Development of a Sign Language*. Exhibition catalog. St. Louis: Washington University Gallery of Art, 1980, pp. 19–20.

JOAN MIRÓ
Peinture, 1925

JOAN MIRÓ
Peinture, 1933

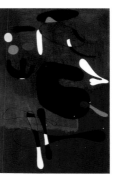

Major Exhibitions

1965   *Miró in St Louis*, City Art Museum (St. Louis, MO)

1980   *Joan Miró: The Development of a Sign Language*, Washington University Gallery of Art (St. Louis, MO); The David and Alfred Smart Gallery, University of Chicago (Chicago, IL)

1980   *Miró: Selected Paintings*, Albright-Knox Art Gallery (Buffalo, NY)

1982   *Miró in America*, Houston Museum of Fine Arts (Houston, TX)

Select Bibliography

Dupin, Jacques. *Miró*. New York: Harry N. Abrams, 1962, p. 527.

Greenberg, Clement. *Joan Miró*. New York: Quadrangle Press, 1948, p. 66, pl. 22.

Hynds, Reed. "Yielding Place to New." *Art News* 45, no. 4 (June 1946), p. 63.

Janson, H. W. "Modern Art in the Washington University Collection." *Bulletin of the City Art Museum of St. Louis* 32, no. 1 (March 1947), no. 16.

———. "The New Art Collection at Washington University." *College Art Journal* 6, no. 3 (Spring 1947), p. 204.

Lubar, Robert S. "Joan Miró, *Peinture* (Painting)." In Ketner, Joseph D., et al. *A Gallery of Modern Art at Washington University in St. Louis*. St. Louis: Washington University Gallery of Art, 1994, pp. 116–17.

Mann, Judith. "Joan Miró: The Development of a Sign Language." Brochure. St. Louis: Washington University Gallery of Art, 1980.

Matthews, J. H. *8 Painters: The Surrealist Context*. Syracuse, NY: Syracuse University Press, 1982, p. 17.

Stich, Sidra. *Joan Miró: The Development of a Sign Language*. Exhibition catalog. St. Louis: Washington University Gallery of Art, 1980, pp. 28–30, fig. 20.

PABLO PICASSO
Glass and Bottle of Suze, 1912

Major Exhibitions

1941   *Picasso Early and Late,* Bignou Gallery (New York, NY)

1946   Title unknown, Bignou Gallery (New York, NY)

1948   *Collage,* Museum of Modern Art (New York, NY)

1949   *The Modern Artist and his World,* Denver Art Museum (Denver, CO); Palace of the Legion of Honor (San Francisco, CA)

1961   *The Art of Assemblage,* Museum of Modern Art (New York, NY); Dallas Museum for Contemporary Art (Dallas, TX); San Francisco Museum of Art (San Francisco, CA)

1967   *Picasso,* Dallas Museum of Fine Arts (Dallas, TX)

1979   *Zeichnungen und Collagen des Kubismus Picasso, Braque, Gris,* Kunsthalle (Bielefeld, Germany)

1980   *Pablo Picasso: A Retrospective,* Museum of Modern Art (New York, NY)

1981   *Master Drawings by Picasso,* Fogg Art Museum, Harvard University (Cambridge, MA)

1981   *Picasso 1881–1973, Esposiçion Antologica,* Museo Española Arte Contemporáneo (Madrid, Spain); Museo Picasso (Barcelona, Spain)

1988   *Aspects of Collage, Assemblage, and the Found Object in Twentieth-Century Art,* Solomon R. Guggenheim Museum (New York, NY)

1989   *Picasso and Braque: Pioneering Cubism,* Museum of Modern Art, (New York, NY)

1992   *Picasso and Things: The Still Lifes of Picasso,* Grand Palais (Paris, France)

Select Bibliography

Apollinare, Guillaume. "Picasso et les Papiers Collés." *Cahiers d'Art* 7, nos. 3, 5 (1932), pp. 117–19.

Boggs, Jean Sutherland. *Picasso and Things.* Exhibition catalog. Cleveland: Cleveland Museum of Art, 1992, p. 112.

–––. "Pablo Picasso, Glass and Bottle of Suze." In Ketner, Joseph D., et al. *A Gallery of Modern Art at Washington University in St. Louis.* St. Louis: Washington University Gallery of Art, 1994, pp.76–77.

Breuning, Margaret. "Tracing the History of Collage." *Art Digest* 23, no. 1 (October 1, 1948), p. 16.

Collage. Exhibition catalog. New York: Museum of Modern Art, 1948.

Cooper, Douglas. *Picasso: Two Concurrent Retrospective Exhibitions.* Exhibition catalog. Fort Worth: Fort Worth Art Center Museum, 1967, p. 32, no. 22.

Cork, Richard. *A Bitter Truth: Avant-Garde and the Great War.* New Haven: Yale University Press, 1994. pp. 21–22.

Cottington, David. *Cubism in the Shadow of War.* New Haven: Yale University Press, 1998, frontispiece, fig.30.

Cranshaw, Roger D. "Notes on Cubism, War and Labour," 1985. In Hertz, Richard, and Norman M. Klein, eds. *Twentieth Century Art Theory: Urbanism, Politics, and Mass Culture.* Englewood Cliffs: Prentice Hall, 1990, pp. 149–56.

Daix, Pierre. *Picasso: The Cubist Years, 1907–1916, A Catalogue Raisonné of the Paintings and Related Works.* London: Thames and Hudson, 1979, p. 289, no. 523, pl. 34.

Frascina, Francis. "Realism and Ideology: An Introduction to Semiotics and Cubism." In Harrison, Charles F., ed. *Primitivism, Cubism, Abstraction: The Early Twentieth Century.* New Haven and London: Yale University Press and The Open University, 1993, pp. 87, 91–95, pl. 77.

Hynds, Reed. "Yielding Place to New." *Art News* 45, no. 4 (June 1946), p. 62.

Janson, H. W. "Modern Art in the Washington University Collection." *Bulletin of the City Art Museum of St. Louis* 32, no. 1 (March 1947), no. 17.

Krauss, Rosalind E., ed. *The Picasso Papers.* New York: Farrar, Strauss, and Giroux, 1998, pp. 26, 40–42, 45, 51, 245 (n. 8), 246 (n. 13), 247 (n. 15).

Leighten, Patricia. "Cubist Anachronisms: Cryptoformalism, Ahistoricity, and Business-as-Usual in New York." *Oxford Art Journal* 17 (1994), pp. 97–99.

–––. *Re-Ordering the Universe: Picasso and Anarchism, 1897–1914.* Princeton: Princeton University Press, 1989, pp. 132, 140, pl. 8, fig. 83.

–––. "Reveil Anarchiste: Salon Painting, Political Satire, Modernist Art." *Modernism/Modernity* 2, no. 2 (April 1995), p. 36.

Richardson, John. *A Life of Picasso, Volume 2: 1907–1917.* New York: Random House, 1996, p. 343.

Rosenblum, Robert. "Picasso and the Typography of Cubism." In *Picasso 1881–1973.* London: Paul Elek, 1973, p. 48, fig. 66.

Rubin, William. *Picasso and Braque: Pioneering Cubism.* Exhibition catalog. New York: Museum of Modern Art, 1989, p. 258.

–––. *Pablo Picasso: A Retrospective.* Exhibition catalog. New York: Museum of Modern Art, 1980, p. 164.

Seitz, William Chapin. *The Art of Assemblage.* Exhibition catalog. New York: Museum of Modern Art, 1961, no. 165, frontispiece.

Tzara, Tristan. "Les Papiers Collés ou le Proverbe en Peinture." *Cahiers d'Art* 6, no. 2 (1931), p 71.

Waldman, Diane. *Collage, Assemblage, and the Found Object.* New York: Harry N. Abrams, 1992, pp. 27–32, pl. 30.

Wescher, Herta. *Picasso: Papiers, Collés. Petite Encyclopédie de l'Art No. 30.* New York: Tudor Publishing, 1960, pl. 4.

Zervos, Christian. *Pablo Picasso, Volume 2.* Paris: Editions Cahiers d'Art, 1942, p. 197, no. 422.

PABLO PICASSO

Les Femmes d'Alger, 1955

Major Exhibitions

1955   *Pablo Picasso*, Galerie Louise Leiris (Paris, France)

1955   *Picasso: Paintings 1900–1955*, Musée des Arts Décoratifs (Paris, France)

1957   *Picasso: 75th Anniversary*, Museum of Modern Art (New York, NY); Art Institute of Chicago (Chicago, IL)

1967   *Picasso Exhibition*, Dallas Museum of Fine Arts (Dallas, TX)

1992   *Picasso: Die Zeit nach Guernica 1937–1973*, Nationalgalerie (Berlin, Germany); Kunsthalle der Hypo-Kulturstiftung (Munich, Germany); Hamburger Kunsthalle (Hamburg, Germany)

1998   *Pablo Picasso and his Personal Collection*, Kunsthalle der Hypo-Kulturstiftung (Munich, Germany)

1999   *Matisse and Picasso: A Gentle Rivalry*, Kimbell Art Museum (Ft. Worth, TX)

2001   *Picasso: Las Grandes Series y Los Maestoros del Pasado (1953–1973)*, Museo Nacional Centro de Arte Reina Sofía

Select Bibliography

Barr, Alfred H., Jr. *Picasso: 75th Anniversary Exhibition*. Exhibition catalog. New York: Museum of Modern Art, 1957, p. 109.

Bernier, Rosamond. *Matisse, Picasso, Miró As I Knew Them*. New York: Knopf, 1991, pp. 156–57.

Boggs, Jean Sutherland. "Pablo Picasso, *Les Femmes d'Alger (Women of Algiers)*." In Ketner, Joseph D., et al. *A Gallery of Modern Art at Washington University in St. Louis*. St. Louis: Washington University Gallery of Art, 1994, pp. 78–79.

Bois, Yve-Alain. *Matisse and Picasso: A Gentle Rivalry*. Exhibition catalog. Ft. Worth and Paris: Kimbell Art Museum and Flammarion, 1998, p. 223, pl. 231.

Leal, Brigitte, et al. *The Ultimate Picasso*. New York: Harry N. Abrams, 2000, pp. 405–408.

O'Brian, Patrick. *Pablo Ruiz Picasso, A Biography*. London: Collins, 1976, pp. 426–27.

Penrose, Roland. *Picasso: His Life and Work*. New York: Harper and Row, 1973, 405–407.

Pablo Picasso. Exhibition catalog. Stockholm: Moderna Museet, 1988, pp. 112, 146.

Picasso: Las Grandes Series. Exhibition catalog. Madrid: Museo Nacional Centro de Arte Reina Sofia and Aldeasa, 2001, pp. 114, 222, 360–61, fig. 8.

Picasso: Paintings 1900–55. Exhibition catalog. Paris: Musée des Arts Décoratifs, 1955, no. 127 N.

Spies, Werner. *Picasso: Die Zeit Nach Guernica 1937–1973*. Exhibition catalog. Stuttgart: Verlag Gerd Hatje GmbH, 1993, p. 115.

Vallentin, Antonina. *Picasso*. New York: Doubleday, 1963, pp. 253–54.

Zervos, Christian. *Pablo Picasso*. Volume 16. Paris: Editions Cahiers d'Art, 1965, p. 133, no. 359.

JACKSON POLLOCK
Sleeping Effort Number 3, 1953

Major Exhibitions

1954 Title unknown, Sidney Janis Gallery (New York, NY) (as *Sleeping Effort*)

1955 *Collector's Choice*, American Federation of Arts (New York, NY), traveling exhibition

1957 *IV Bienal de Museu de Arte Moderna–U.S. Section* (Sao Paolo, Brazil)

1964 *Jackson Pollock*, Marlborough-Gerson Gallery (New York, NY)

1967 Title unknown, Museum of Modern Art (New York, NY); Los Angeles County Museum of Art (Los Angeles, CA)

Select Bibliography

Hess, Thomas B. "Jackson Pollock." *Art News* 53, no.1 (March 1954) (as *Quiet Effort*), p. 41.

Kagan, Andrew. "Jackson Pollock, *Sleeping Effort Number 3*." In Ketner, Joseph D., et al. *A Gallery of Modern Art at Washington University in St. Louis*. St. Louis: Washington University Gallery of Art, 1994, pp. 174–75.

O'Connor, Francis Valentine. *Jackson Pollock*. Exhibition catalog. New York: Museum of Modern Art, 1967, pp. 69–70.

O'Connor, Francis Valentine, and Eugene Victor Thaw, eds. *Pollock: A Catalogue Raisonné of Paintings, Drawings, and Other Works*. New Haven: Yale University Press, 1978, no. 373.

O'Hara, Frank. *Jackson Pollock*. New York: George Braziller, 1959, p. 30, pl.74.

Jackson Pollock: 1912-1956. Exhibition catalog. New York: Marlborough-Gerson Gallery, 1964, no. 143.

Robertson, Bryan. *Jackson Pollock*. New York: Harry N. Abrams, 1960, pp. 52, 149, pl. 160.

YVES TANGUY
La Tour Marine, 1944

Major Exhibitions

1945   *Paintings by Yves Tanguy*, Pierre Matisse Gallery (New York, NY)

1955   *Yves Tanguy Retrospective*, Museum of Modern Art (New York, NY)

1961   *Magritte-Tanguy Retrospective*, Museum of Modern Art (New York, NY), traveling exhibition

1963   *Yves Tanguy: A Summary of his Works*, Pierre Matisse Gallery (New York, NY)

1967   *Twentieth Century American Painting*, Grand Rapids Art Museum (Grand Rapids, MI)

Select Bibliography

Breuning, Margaret. "The Surrealist Delusion of Yves Tanguy." *Art Digest* 19, no. 16 (May 15, 1945), p. 9.

Haftmann, Werner. *Painting in the 20th Century*, Volume 2. New York: Frederick A. Praeg, 1965, no. 552.

Hynds, Reed. "Yielding Place to New." *Art News* 45, no. 4 (June 1946), p. 63.

Janson, H. W. "Modern Art in the Washington University Collection." *Bulletin of the City Art Museum of St. Louis* 32, no. 1 (March 1947), no. 21.

Nessen, Susan. "Yves Tanguy, *La Tour Marine* (*Tower of the Sea*)." In Ketner, Joseph D., et al. *A Gallery of Modern Art at Washington University in St. Louis*. St. Louis: Washington University Gallery of Art, 1994, pp. 120–21.

Soby, James Thrall. *Magritte-Tanguy*. Exhibition catalog. New York: Museum of Modern Art, 1955, p. 50.

Yves Tanguy: A Summary of his Works. Exhibition catalog. New York: Pierre Matisse Gallery, 1963, p. 153, no. 333.

Twentieth Century American Painting. Exhibition catalog. Grand Rapids: Grand Rapids Art Museum, 1967, p. 24.

THEO VAN DOESBURG
Composition VII: The Three Graces,
1917

Major Exhibitions

1917 *Tentoonstelling van Schilderyen,* Pavilion (Domburg, Germany)

1922 Title unknown, Städtisches Museum (Weimar, Germany)

1922 One-man show, Hannover Quader Club (Hannover, Germany)

1935 *Société des Artistes Indépendants. 46me Exposition,* Grand Palais des Champs-Elysées (Paris, France)

1936 *Theo van Doesburg,* Stedelijk Museum (Amsterdam)

1936 *Cubism and Abstract Art,* Museum of Modern Art (New York, NY)

1937 *Konstruktivisten,* Kunsthalle (Basel, Switzerland)

1945 *Art Concret,* Galerie René Drouin (Paris, France)

1946 Title unknown, Palais de l'Art Moderne (Paris, France)

1947 *Theo van Doesburg: Retrospective Exhibition,* Art of This Century Gallery (New York, NY)

1966 *From Daumier to Pollock,* William Rockhill Nelson Gallery of Art - Mary Atkins Museum of Art (Kansas City, MO)

1968 *Theo van Doesburg 1883-1931,* venue unknown (Eindoven, The Netherlands); venue unknown (The Hague, The Netherlands)

1969 *Theo van Doesburg 1883-1931,* Kunsthalle Nürnberg (Nürnberg, Germany); Kunsthalle Basel (Basel, Switzerland)

1992 *Green Acres: Neocolonialism in the U.S.,* Washington University Gallery of Art (St. Louis, MO)

1994 *La Beauté Exacte: Art Pays Bas Xième Siecle, De Van Gogh à Mondrian,* Musée d'Art Moderne de la Ville de Paris (Paris, France)

2000 *Theo van Doesburg,* Centraal Museum (Utrecht, The Netherlands); Kröller Müiler Museum (Otterlo, The Netherlands)

Select Bibliography

Aggis, Maurice, and Peter Jones. "Van Doesburg: A Continuing Inspiration." *Studio International* 177 (March 1969), pp. 113–16.

La Beauté Exacte. Exhibition catalog. Paris: Le Musée d'Art Moderne de la Ville de Paris, 1994, p. 241.

Blotkamp, Carel. "Theo van Doesburg." In Loeb, Charlotte I., and Arthur L. Loeb, eds. *De Stijl: The Formative Years, 1917–1922.* Cambridge, MA: The MIT Press, 1986, pp. 22, 37.

Cubism and Abstract Art. Exhibition catalog. New York: Museum of Modern Art and Arno Press, 1936, p. 208.

Hoek, Els, et al. *Theo van Doesburg: Oeuvre Catalogue.* Utrecht: Centraal Museum, 2000, pp. 195–96, fig. 552.

Illustrated Checklist of the Collection: Paintings, Sculpture and Works on Paper. St. Louis: Washington University Gallery of Art, 1981, pp. 30–31.

Janson, H. W. "Modern Art in the Washington University Collection." *Bulletin of the City Art Museum of St. Louis* 32, no. 1 (March 1947), no. 7.

Joosten, J. M. "Rondon van Doesburg. De Schilder - en Beeldhouwkunst Binnen het Verband van De Stijl; 1915-1922. Het Werk van Theo van Doesburg, Piet Mondrian, Bart van der Leck, en Vilmos Huszar." *Tableau* 5, no.1 (September–October 1982), p. 57.

Lemoine, S. *Theo van Doesburg: Peinture, Architecture, Théorie.* Paris: Sers, 1990, p. 86.

Polano, S. *Theo van Doesburg: Scritti di Arte e di Achitettura.* Rome: Officina, 1979, p. 526, no. 110, fig. 51.

Troy, Nancy J. "Theo van Doesburg, *Composition VII: The Three Graces.*" In Ketner, Joseph D., et al. *A Gallery of Modern Art at Washington University in St. Louis.* St. Louis: Washington University Gallery of Art, 1994, pp. 104–105.

Welsh, R. P. "Theo van Doesburg and German Abstraction." In Bulhof, F. *Nijhoff, van Ostaijen, De Stijl: Modernism in the Netherlands and Belgium in the First 1/4 of the 20th Century.* The Hague, 1976, pp. 83–84, fig. 12.